GW00645542

Arseblog Presents:

SO PADDY GOT UP

'Bejesus,' said Paddy 'I sang it so well,
I think I'll get up and I'll sing it again!'
So Paddy got up and he sang it again,
Over and over and over again.
'Bejesus,' said Paddy 'I sang it so well,
I think I'll get up and I'll sing it again!'
So Paddy got up and he sang it again,
Over and over and over again.
(repeat to fade)

Arsenal fans – traditional

Arseblog Presents:

SO PADDY
GOT UP

EDITED BY
ANDREW MANGAN

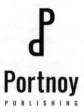

Portnoy
PUBLISHING

To Mrs Blogs, for understanding

First published in 2011 by Portnoy Publishing

2 – Hardback, Jan 2012 Reprint Edition

Copyright © arseblog.com and the contributors, 2011.
The Authors have asserted their moral rights.

The right of Andrew Mangan to be identified as the Author of the work has been
asserted by him in accordance with the Copyright, Designs and Patents Act 1988.

All rights reserved. No part of this publication may be reproduced, stored in a retrieval
system, or transmitted in any form or by means, electronic, mechanical, photocopying,
recording or otherwise, without prior and express permission of the publishers.

This book is sold subject to the condition that it shall not, by way of trade or
otherwise, be circulated in any form or binding other than that in which it is published.

ISBN: 978 0 956981 34 9

Printed and bound by CPI Group (UK) Ltd., Croydon, CR0 4YY

Cover design: David Rudnick
Typeset in: Adobe Garamond by Saltwater Publishing, Dublin

Portnoy Publishing
PO Box 12093, Dublin 6, Ireland.
www.portnoypublishing.com
Twitter: @portnoypub

LINE UP

1

IN THE BEGINNING

ANDREW MANGAN

'HOW DO YOU WRITE A BLOG EVERY DAY FOR 10 YEARS?'

Well, it's quite simple. You get up every morning. You go to the bathroom, after which you make coffee, you take said coffee to your office upstairs/across the hall/in the back bedroom (location has changed due to various house moves), and you sit down and write it. Depending on seasons/location you work wearing a dressing gown and slippers or shorts and flip-flops (this is what I call the Dublin/Barcelona dichotomy). You do that 7 days a week, 52 weeks a year, for nigh on ten years and it becomes something of a habit; part of your routine. If you wake in the morning with a bladder that needs emptying, soon enough you wake up with a head that needs emptying. Not of piss, thankfully. That would suggest a serious leak or some badly plumbed pipes. But essentially that's how. You sit, you drink coffee, you scour the morning papers (well, their websites), you flooter around on NewsNow, perhaps a bit of Google News, lately a bit of Twitter, and then you bash it out. Spell check it, still miss a few errors, wait for le correction, and publish. Simple.

'WHY HAVE YOU WRITTEN A BLOG EVERY DAY FOR TEN YEARS?'

Well, because I found a subject matter I love, because, as I explained above, my head needs to metaphorically (no Redknappian 'literally' here) piss out words, and because I really love doing it. Ok, there are some mornings when I might have taken a drink the night before when I don't exactly feel full of the joys of spring, but I could count on one hand the amount of times I've opened an eye and said 'Mrs Blogs, there are about 513 things I'd rather do now than write a blog'. And you know me, being a moderate drinker at the best of times, it tends to affect me if I have more than a couple of halves of shandy. Or halves of bottles of Havana Club.

The why, back then, was because it was something new, interesting, exciting and which allowed me to write. The why now, well, I write a blog because that's what I do. Some people have peculiar talents. Contortionists, for example, who can pick their nose with their toes, or that bloke who was in that freaky circus and discovered that he was able to lift heavy weights which were attached by a hook to his scrotum. Don't ask me how he discovered this was his talent, but I find it unlikely that Scrotumy Joe had a moment of serendipity when his life's calling was made clear to him. What I do might not be as niche as those two but after forty years on this earth I've realised the thing I'm best at is writing a blog about Arsenal. So that's why I do it.

'OK, BUT WHAT MADE YOU WRITE A BLOG ABOUT ARSENAL IN THE FIRST PLACE?'

Ah, here's where it gets interesting. In so much as a condensed version of four years of my life can be interesting. We have to go back in time a bit, to late 1997. At the time I was a DJ, amongst other things. Not a particularly great DJ, I'll admit, but I could slap together a few hours of bouncy house tunes with only the odd horrendous, beat clashing mix. So, my friend Daragh called.

'Do you fancy doing a gig this evening?'

'Well, I was going to sit around connect to this Internet thing with my spanking new 28.8k modem but sure go on then'.

'Right, I'll pick you up later. One more thing, you're from Ibiza'.

'I am?'

'Yeah, we sold tickets saying some cool DJ from Ibiza was coming'.

'Who?'

'We just made up a name'

'What name?'

'Jon 'The Mixinator' Jonson'.

'Ah here …'

'Seriously'.

'Fucks sake'.

'So you're him'.

'You're an awful spoofer, you know'.

'Pick you up around 9'.

So, I got my records together, thought of something to say when the first person said 'You know, for a DJ from Ibiza you're not very tanned, are you?' and soon we arrived at the venue. A suburban nightclub more used to 'Sing Hallelujah' and bottles of Ritz than a load of pilled-up, face the DJ merchants who would stop occasionally to gasp 'water … water …' for fear of over-heating and dropping dead.

I should have known the night was going to be bad when I set up the Technics and tried to plug them in. It being 1997, and at that time the height of modernity, the plugs were standard. You know, square pinned. The plug sockets, however, had obviously been installed some time in the late '50s and accepted only round plugs.

'I think we might have a small problem here', I said to Daragh.

'Have you got any CDs?' he asked, looking at the two nicely-plugged in CD decks.

'I think I have a copy of Brothers in Arms at home but that's not much use to us here'.

'Oh fuck', he said.

'Yeah.'

Quite how the situation was resolved, I don't remember. I have vague recollections of standing around drinking things until someone found a late night hardware store – not easy to come by in 1997, let me tell you – or we cut the plugs off the CD decks and attached them to the record players. Anyway, despite the round-pinned plugs, the gig was fine. I don't think anyone asked me why I was so milky for an Ibiza-based DJ as I stood there and played records until 2am or so. Not quite as seminal as Sasha at Renaissance or anything but generally fine and I pocketed a whopping £40 for my night's work (hey, back then you could buy a nice suit, go on a foreign holiday and still have enough left over for a night at pictures with that kind of money).

The problems started on the way home. I was in the front seat as Daragh drove me back to my house on the South Circular Road. We came to a crossroads, complete with handy traffic lights so you knew it was your turn to go. Traffic was light, as you'd expect at that time of night. In fact, there were only two cars on the road – us and another man heading in the opposite direction. As we went through the lights, which were green, he decided this would be the perfect time to turn right. It wasn't. The perfect time would have been when we weren't halfway across the junction. The perfect time would have ensured that he didn't crash right into us, exploding the airbag in Daragh's face and leaving me completely unscathed apart from a hideously broken arm and most of the windshield in my forehead. I got out of the car imploring somebody to commit an act of unspeakable violence on the other man before I noticed my second elbow. It hurt. Anyway, the ambulance came and brought me to hospital, where they X-rayed me, picked as much of the glass out of my head as they could, and left me sitting on a trolley in a room off the emergency department. Surgery was to take place the next morning.

Mrs Blogs arrived at the hospital and I asked the nurse if it might be possible to have something for the pain.

'Sure,' she said. 'But you'll have to stand up and undo your pants'.

I went to an all boys school run by priests so was immediately suspicious but figured I didn't have much choice.

'This,' said the nurse, 'is just the legal side of heroin.' She then jabbed me in the arse with a giant needle. I know people tut-tut at drug addicts but at that precise moment my intense love of morphine was born. It's almost worth really hurting yourself just so you can get some. Soon the pain was replaced by a warm glow, I recall telling Mrs Blogs about how the stupid nightclub only had round plugs.

'Can you believe that? In this day and age, round plugs?'

'I certainly found it hard to believe the first few times you told me,' she said nicely. And from then it was a slow drift off into nothingness. I woke in the morning, on the trolley, pants still not done up properly, having slept for hours sitting up straight. God bless you sweet delicious morphine.

SO, THE ACCIDENT CHANGED YOUR LIFE SO MUCH YOU DECIDED TO WRITE ABOUT ARSENAL?

Hold your horses! There's still a way to go yet. Suffice to say I didn't take being badly injured well. Especially when after three months of weekly visits to the hospital, wearing a shoulder to wrist cast, a doctor calmly announced, 'Your arm is still broken.' This was no surprise to me as I'd been telling them this for weeks in my out-patient visits.

'I think my arm is still broken,' I would say.

'Don't be silly.'

'No, really. When I lie in bed at night I can crunch the two broken bits of bone off each other.'

'You are being silly,' the doctor would reply.

'Well, you're the doctor, I suppose.'

Turns out he was a bit of a shit doctor and when a better doctor took a look at the X-rays he was happy to conclude that my arm was indeed still broken and required surgery. This was depressing news but there you go. I went in for surgery, they sliced my arm open from shoulder to elbow, put in a metal plate, some screws, closed me up and gave me some more morphine for a few days. It was a during a blissed-out haze I watched us beat Chelsea at Stamford Bridge on the TV in the room they gave me (I think out of guilt at being so crap earlier). Stephen Hughes scored both goals that day. Anyway, my arm was sort of fixed. I had to get the stitches out, learn how to bend it again, and all that other awful physio stuff. Yet the worst was still to come. Broken bones, second elbows, busted heads, glassy bits finding their way to the surface of my skin months later, surgery, rehab and all that paled into insignificance when I hurtled through the windscreen of life into ... middle management.

I had spent the previous years of my life working as a DJ, sound engineer and voice-over bloke, but after the accident and a grand total of nine months out of action I had to get a job. I lied my way into AOL as tech support agent. That was fun. The call-centre for the UK was based in Dublin.

'Hello, I can't sign up with this AOL software.'

[Insert 20 minutes of installing, reinstalling, removing and adding back the TCP/IP control panel, rebooting computers, modems, toasters, anything you can think of. Then brainwave!]

'Excuse me, madam. Can you please tell me your address?'

'It's 52 Flotheringtominham Crescent, Scunthorpe, County –'

'There's your problem!' I'd say.

'What? My address?'

'Yes, you see the AOL software has powerful anti-swear-ing software. It doesn't like part of your address.'

'Which part?'

'Erm, the bit between the S and the H ...'

'You mean...? Oh! Eeek, Clive, you should hear what this awful Irishman almost made me say.'

And that was the highlight of a life in technical support. A move to Ireland's national telecoms company and a job as a team leader/middle manager guy didn't make things much better. On the one hand I rarely had to speak to anyone who had a tech support problem, on the other I only got to speak to really, really angry people. And then there were team meetings, team building, management meetings, stats, spreadsheets, and a seemingly never-end-ing procession of stupid things and stupid people who existed solely to make my life miserable. Anyway, it got to the point where I would come home from work, sit out the back garden having a smoke (not of morphine sadly), and gaze fondly at the sky at passing planes. In fact, I would spend a lot of time gazing fondly at planes, wanting to be on them. And I hate flying. That's how bad it was.

Anyway, long story short, me and Mrs Blogs decided to move to Spain. We'd sell our house, pack our stuff, pets and Blogette up, and move to a medium-sized town just out-side Barcelona. No, we did not speak any Spanish beyond ordering calamari and various cocktails, but that was of no great worry. We decided to do the sensible thing; we'd make it up as we went along.

Fast forward to Barcelona airport in August 2001. Mrs Blogs and I are standing at the luggage carousel awaiting our various baggage. People are shuffling around, doing that thing they do to get as close as they can to the plastic flaps which birth the bags into their new realm, and we're standing waiting, for we know what is to come. The carousel starts up, suitcases of all kinds start to appear, people are clutching greedily at them as if everyone else on the flight is David Hillier. And shortly afterwards our stuff emerges. There's a sequence. It goes: suitcase > small bag > suitcase > cat > suitcase > basset hound > suitcase > suitcase > cat > cat > suitcase … well, you can imagine.

The first thing Opus, the basset, did when he got outside the airport was stop and do an enormous poo on the zebra crossing outside the airport. An inauspicious start to life in Spain, but considering how the relationship between Arsenal and FC Barcelona was to develop down the years perhaps you might say it was prophetic.

OK, SO YOU GOT TO SPAIN AND YOU STARTED AN ARSENAL BLOG? PLEASE. I CAN'T TAKE ANYMORE OF THIS.

Yes. And no. Sorry. After all that time with spreadsheets (hold me) I decided it would be good to take some time off. So I did. We got there in August and Arseblog started in February. In that time I spent every day on the telephone to telecoms company, Terra, trying to have ADSL installed. I ordered it in August; it arrived some time in the new year. I can't remember exactly when, all I know is that it was the longest, most frustrating time of my life. You know when you take a trip to the dentist and the time in the chair crawls? Well, this was a bazillion and fifty times worse. I spoke little or no Spanish, but they did have an English-speaking department. In retrospect I think 'department' might be pushing it. It consisted of one woman. She got to know me quite well.

'Oh please,' I'd say. 'When are you going to install my Internet?'

'Eet weel be berry, berry soon. I promise!'

2 months later

'Oh please,' I'd say. 'When are you going to install my Internet?'

'Eet weel be berry, berry soon. I promise!'

Eventually a man came, frowned at my Mac and spent two hours trying to get it online. Soon, however, I had the worldwide web at my fingertips. And at lightning speed too. 512kb! Blimey. It was the Ben Johnson of Internet when you're used to dial-up. It changed my life, I'll admit it. Well, it meant I could load web pages faster and at the end of the day, isn't that all any of us want? It opened up a new world of websites and soon I chanced upon these odd things called 'blogs': personal websites, updated on a regular basis, which seemed to be about nothing in particular, and yet they were strangely compelling. Really, what did I care about a lady who kept bunny rabbits in Cambridge? Nothing. Except I found myself clicking back to her Blogspot site. Everywhere I looked, there were blogs.

At the time, I had a very small and rather shit hosting company. I basically re-sold web-space in packages to people and raked in amazing amounts of up to $5 a month from some customers. I decided that to further augment this income I should look into the design side of things. That's where you could make the big money. And once you got the money, you got the power, and then the women. Except I only wanted the money…and maybe a bit of power. Anyway, the main problem was I wasn't very good at it. Not bad either, but not great. I could cobble something together, but if you want artistic, fresh and funky, I'm not your guy. If I were an interior designer you'd get a lot of magnolia and a print on the wall of that guy sitting in front of the TV with the TV blowing his hair back. I tried though. To kick things off I thought I'd make a website which would be a bit funny. So was born 'The Church of Bob', an odd effort which revolved around the premise that Robert Pires was not *only* the messiah but an Internet evangelist who was trying to shill people via a donation scam. As you can imagine the appeal was somewhat limited.

I needed something else, something different; something that would last. It struck me that I needed a website I could continuously update, a blog! To do a blog continuously it had to be something that, a) I was interested in, and b) had plenty of material. I could think only of one thing but then I worried about what my family would say if they discovered my penchant for leprous, dwarf, panther porn. Then it struck me. Arsenal, a blog about Arsenal. And what else could you call a blog about Arsenal only ... Arseblog.

RIGHT, WELL THANKS FOR THAT! IT'S BEEN A PLEASURE BUT MUST DASH, I'VE GOT TO SEE A MAN ABOUT A -

Wait right there. I'm not finished yet.

AWWWW.

So you see, without that car crash in 1997 there probably would be no Arseblog. I don't know who that crap driver was, but you wouldn't be reading this without him. Life can take you in strange directions. I think Arseblog was the very first Arsenal blog. There were other Arsenal websites at the time, Rupert Ward's, Arseweb, the granddaddy of them all and Chris Parry's, Arsenal World. There was Boring Boring Arsenal, by the wonderfully named Richard Head. Our old friend at Arsenal News Review might claim to have invented blogging whilst smoking super-hemp in a teepee with The Moody Blues, but a blog needs interaction and comments to be worthy of the name. There was also this site called @ FC, the Red Geezer, who wrote the most incredibly biting and funny match reports. It would be a lie to say his ability to look at Arsenal with passion and humour wasn't an influence. Around the time I started Arseblog he stopped writing his site. Maybe I was in the right place at the right time to fill the gap he left behind. Whoever you are, Red Geezer, if I had a cap, my cap would be doffed to you. I have a nice hat though so I'll doff that instead.

Some of those sites are still around and some have gone by the wayside, but many, many more have come along and I don't think it'd be wrong of me to suggest there are more blogs about Arsenal than about any other Premier League team. In fact, I'd put a cheeky bet on there being more blogs about Arsenal than there are about any other subject in the world. Ever. Whatever your disposition, beliefs, loyalties, demands, predilections, nationality, locality or anything else you can think of, there's something for everyone. We may not agree with some of them, or like some of them; but here's the great thing about the Internet, nobody is forcing you to read something you don't like. You don't even need an off button; you just don't go there in the first place.

Over the years, through the blog and the Arsecast, I've come to know many of these Arsenal bloggers. What is fantastic is the vast majority of them do what they do simply out of a love of Arsenal Football Club. For no reward, and on a daily basis they have provided wonderful, timeless, free content for other Arsenal fans to chew over. I don't think people realise quite how much work that takes, especially when it's done in spare time. Joining them in these pages are some writers of a more professional bent who will be well known to readers of Arseblog. Collectively, they have entertained me, moved me, informed me, made me laugh, made me feel sympathy, empathy, anger, guilt, passion, rage, delight and all the other emotions that we get from football itself. The following pages will, I hope, do the same to you, as this unique collection of writing about Arsenal Football Club looks at everything from the club's humble origins to where it finds itself today, from great players to great managers, from tactics to fans to stadia to kits, amongst many other things. It is my absolute pleasure to present this book to you.

I hope it's one that you can read, the same way Paddy sang, over and over and over again.

Andrew Mangan writes Arseblog.com, the award-winning Arsenal blog founded in 2002. Quite happily married to Mrs Blogs, he is firmly convinced Robert Pires is the dreamiest man on earth.

2

ONE GEORGIE GRAHAM

AMY LAWRENCE

It was just after lunch on the 21st of February 1994 when the news broke. At the time the Arsenal Stadium was being set up for an evening match. As the stock at the Gunners Shop was being filled, the match programmes delivered, the turnstiles unlocked, the kit laid out in the dressing room, the flowers in the colours of the visitors displayed in the marble halls, a whacking great red and white bombshell dropped onto Highbury. George Graham's time at Arsenal was up. Unceremoniously, brutally, up.

With a little bit of distance and perspective it shouldn't really have been such a seismic shock. Results wise, the team was in free-fall and stood a mere four points above the relegation zone (the last 12 games produced dismal statistics: W1 D5 L6). Performance wise, the players appeared to be trudging through treacle. Spirit wise, Arsenal had been trapped in a limbo of uncertainty for months as the bung scandal, in which Graham stood accused of dipping his hands in the till by accepting irregular payments from a Norwegian agent by the name of Rune Hauge, was under investigation. So when George was finally ushered towards the exit, we should not have felt so stunned. So bewildered. Yet as the crowds descended upon Highbury for a league game against Nottingham Forest, and opened up their match programmes to see George's face and read George's words of wisdom (it was obviously too late to change anything) the overwhelming feeling was one of loss.

For all of George's imperfections – and apart from the obvious brown envelope episode he had undeniably allowed a decline to take hold – he had been in many ways the perfect Arsenal manager. As an ex-player, and part of the 1971 double winning team, his emotional ties to the club were strongly bound. As an Arsenal historian (his study at home was dedicated to the club's past), he was proud to uphold the traditions set by Herbert Chapman, Bertie Mee et al. As a manager, he was motivated, shrewd and strategic enough to build a team capable of producing extraordinary winning moments. With his suave repartee and smart cannoned blazer, he represented Arsenal magnificently. On that day when he was dismissed, with the bookies taking bets on his replacement naming the likes of Steve Coppell, David Pleat and Walter Smith as frontrunners, alongside some club stalwarts without the big time coaching experience, the predominant feeling amongst the fans was this: Never again could any manager at Highbury possibly be so "Arsenal".

Across London, in the office of a football magazine, a cub reporter, enjoying a debut season in the job of watching football for a living, assessed the news. The editor took one look at the cub reporter, who was clearly struggling to concentrate on anything.

"Go home, Amy," the editor said.

Okay, I'll admit, it wasn't my most professional moment, but to fans of a certain age, who grew up with George's team, who experienced the profound effects of White Hart Lane 87, Anfield 89, Highbury 91, Wembley 93 and Copenhagen 94 whilst they were still learning about life, the universe and everything, the sacking of the mastermind was an enormous deal. Everyone around the place was shaken. Record goalscorer Ian Wright confessed to being "deeply disappointed". Goalkeeping coach Bob Wilson called it "terribly sad". And frustrating too, adding, "He's going to be labelled for the rest of his career when everyone else in football knows that label could be alongside 20 or 30 other people." That George was the fall guy when the culture of "unsolicited gifts", as he called it, was prevalent, must have cut him even deeper.

Ironically, the act of cutting clever transfer deals – one of his undeniable strengths in creating successful teams – ultimately proved his downfall. John Jensen and Pal Lydersen, two players delivered to Arsenal by Hauge, did not turn out to be the Scot's most ingenious pieces of business. The fact George paid back the £425,000 Hauge had given him was not, in the end, enough of a defence. It was over. Arsenal beat Forest 1-0 that night. Chris Kiwomya scored the only goal. The crowd went home to take it all in and wonder where on earth Arsenal would go from here.

Such are the cycles in the life of a football club. One man's demise is another's opportunity, and, after a couple of caretakers and a season of Bruce Rioch, a certain Arsene Wenger walked into the Marble Halls, full of his own ideas and expectations. That was the very journey taken by George in 1986. Arsenal had been drifting. After Don Howe's spell in charge came to a sorry end, Steve Burtenshaw stepped in to look after the team for a couple of months. The Arsenal board were on the hunt for a new leader. George, a young coach with a reputation for having a tough edge, was on a shortlist of four. As an Arsenal man he was the first to be interviewed. The board never bothered to meet the other three candidates.

The George Graham who strode back into Highbury was a very different animal to the Stroller, as he was nicknamed in his playing days. Gorgeous George, the player, had a luxury style on the pitch and an eye for the good life off it. Mister Graham the manager was ready to crack down on exactly the kind of player he had been. He liked stars, but only 'performing' stars. He expected dedication, desire, and discipline. On arriving at London Colney he noted that a couple of the more flamboyant players, Charlie Nicholas and Graham Rix, had pierced ears. "If you want to wear an earring it's compulsory to wear a dress," he quipped. Point made.

George printed out one of his favourite quotes, from the legendary American Football coach Vince Lombardi, about the three essential components to winning: technique, discipline, and team spirit. He quickly noticed that some of the senior pros in the team were not so strong on the discipline side. Drinking clubs and gambling groups came with the territory in 1980's football in England. If the slightest reluctance to knuckle down and break a few bad habits was evident, George had no qualms about letting a player go, regardless of status. Renowned internationals like Nicholas, Rix and Kenny Sansom moved on. George began to build his team around a group of hungry young players (Adams, Rocastle, Thomas, Merson) and bargain buys (Dixon, Bould, Winterburn, Smith) with everything to prove.

A new resilience was born; a never-say-die mentality was fostered. It all began with the legendary back four, formed by relentless drilling on the training field. George used to deliberately outnumber his defence, playing 4 v 6 to push them and test them until they could recite the mantra "clean sheets" in their sleep. As George once joked, "Even the bulbs in my garden were in formation."

The manager's insatiable appetite for winning rubbed off, and team spirit soared. In the words of the late, great, David Rocastle, they "fought for each other like blood brothers."

It was never going to happen, but what marvels could have been achieved in recent seasons had George been summoned by Arsene to sort out that defence and inject a large dose of resilience.

Arsenal's successes under George were so emotionally charged and dramatically delivered we sometimes wondered who was writing these scripts. The Littlewoods Cup in 1987 came after a humdinger of a semi-final, won at the death, in the lair of the old enemy at Tottenham. The first league championship in 18 years was the most improbable finish to a title race ever seen, with the underdogs so dismissed it seemed like a waste of time even boarding the coach to Anfield in 89, only for deliverance to come in stoppage time of the entire season. Two years later Arsenal were the nearly-invincibles, losing only one game en route to the finishing line, despite the blows of a two point deduction for a brawl at Old Trafford and losing their captain for two months when Tony Adams was imprisoned for drink driving. Then came the Cup collection, with a domestic double clinched in the final seconds of extra time in the 1993 FA Cup final, and the Cup Winners Cup won against all odds with a classic one nil to the Arsenal in 1994.

Six trophies in eight years; three of them won with late goals; four of them coming from losing or unfancied positions. All of them requiring the blend of technique, discipline and team-spirit. A banner was unfurled from the Clock End boxes as Arsenal were champions in 1991: "George Knows".

His reign was not without criticism, however. The old 'boring Arsenal' tag was hooked on to his team. That was a particularly harsh assessment of many of the classy ball players he used – Limpar, Rocastle and Wright were anything *but* boring – but nobody could deny things were going stale towards the end. As Tony Adams put it, "Our league football was dreadful, I think we were in a bit of schtuck."

George himself always thought his team deserved more respect. "Yes, winning is boring, isn't it?" he pouted.

History has not been kind to George. The fact he was eventually followed by the doubles and delicious football devised by Wenger and televised with all the razzmatazz of Sky and the Premiership, together with the notion that he left in disgrace because of the bung scandal, means his achievements are sometimes glossed over. More's the pity. They deserve to be cherished to the full.

When Sir Alex Ferguson was being lauded for Manchester United's record 19th title, the quote about "knocking Liverpool off their perch" was referenced liberally. But it wasn't Ferguson who initially defeated the dynasty at Anfield. It was George who delivered the first body blows. It was George who made the serial trophy collectors, the team that had dominated the 70's and 80's, wobble and lose their footing at the top of the English game. At the time of his departure George had lost his way. Whether he could have rebuilt his team time and again, as Ferguson did, is one for pure hypothesis. But he is entitled to wonder what might have been.

The comparison with Ferguson also works in the sense that George was the last Arsenal manager able to oversee absolutely every detail of the club and its workforce. No matter how small your contribution to the running of Arsenal, George wanted to know you, and keep you motivated for the cause.

As a teenager, I used to have a holiday job at Highbury working in the Gunners Shop. It was a homely little place plonked onto the side of the Clock End – you could probably fit about 30 of them into the footprint of the Armoury – and was famously run for years by ex-keeper, Jack Kelsey. It was common for fans to work part-time at Highbury then. You could get a season ticket in exchange for a few days painting the crash barriers on the North Bank or touching up the exit gates.

One summer's day George caused quite a flutter in the Gunners Shop by swanning in quite unannounced, having a chat about the items on display and how much they cost, and asking each of us shop-girls about ourselves. As if we couldn't get any giddier, an ice cream van pulled up outside on Avenell Road and George gave us a wink. "Come on girls, I'll buy you all an ice cream."

As we waited for our 99's, somebody from the flats above took aim at George with an egg. They missed. Egg landed all over a passing lady with her shopping. "Must have been a Tottenham fan," muttered George, before he went to empathise with the now eggy lady and find out if she needed some help.

On so many levels a similar scene is impossible to imagine today. Arsene Wenger could not possibly keep up with the cast of thousands that work in and around the club now. It would be most unusual to find him wandering around the different departments, trying to find out how people are doing and what they are up to in the good name of Arsenal. Significantly, George did it not only because he could, but because he wanted to.

The history of Arsenal Football Club should never dare to understate his era. There really was only one Georgie Graham.

Amy Lawrence is a football writer for the Guardian and Observer and a daily reader of Arseblog for obvious reasons.

3

THE ARSENAL: FROM OPEN SEWERS TO OPEN SANDWICHES

TIM STILLMAN

In the summer of 2011, Arsenal F.C. undertook a lucrative pre-season tour to Malaysia and China. Whilst the primary reason for the tour was commercial, it did bring the club face-to-face with a branch of the club's support that they could only have had a cerebral appreciation for previously. Arsene Wenger seemed to imply that the Premier League's sparkly dime had informed this colonial phenomenon, "The Premier League has penetrated in Asia." Arsene is not at all incorrect to make that connection, but it's also a continuation of a theme that has persisted at the club throughout its 125-year history. Based, as the club have been, in their suburban garrison womb of Woolwich and the cosmopolitan borough of Islington, Arsenal have been something of a cultural beacon. Many different ethnic strands have identified with Arsenal and woven themselves into its fabric.

A typical match-day at the Emirates will reflect this milieu. But, unsurprisingly, the embryonic years of Woolwich Arsenal weren't quite as diverse. At the club's inception, the fan base was plucked from the same nest as the playing staff – the armoury workhouses of Dial Square and the Royal Arsenal East factory opposite Plumstead Station. Plumstead was very much a garrison town, so Squaddies and munitions workers largely comprised the Manor Ground terraces: hard men living hard lives. The Woolwich Arsenal support revelled in their status as pariahs. The Manor Ground was positioned next to the Southern Outfall Sewer; meaning effluent was frequently streamed under the spectators' hobnailed boots. An industrial works provided a further dystopian backdrop, billowing out a putrid cocktail of yellowy chemicals. Opposition supporters would often refer to the club as coming "from the sinister factory," due to its high walls, which aroused suspicion in outsiders.

The supporters brought their factory camaraderie into the ground with them. Contemporary journalists would often complain bitterly about the coarse language adopted by the Woolwich Arsenal fans – most unbecoming in Victorian England. In scenes far removed from today's more genteel, middle-class environs, the 1892-93 season saw Woolwich Arsenal have one match abandoned and one severely interrupted as fans made their way onto the pitch to assault hapless referees. The lack of adequate facilities at the Manor

Ground often meant men just urinated where they stood on the terracing. This hybrid of crudeness, together with the ground's scarce accessibility by public transport, moved a journalist from the Liverpool Star to refer to matches at Woolwich Arsenal as "the annual trip to Hell." Reports of heavy drinking amongst fans and players after home games became folklore in the Royal Oak – the hostelry in which the club was founded. In the club's early years, with Association Football still a Northern-centric pursuit, Woolwich Arsenal and its fans were considered the unwanted stepchild of English football. In the eyes of the Victorian Sports press, they were a side of brutes playing physical unattractive football, to an uncouth mob of working class labourers.

Of course by 1910, upwardly mobile proprietor and Conservative MP Henry Norris had taken over the club and recognised that, to survive the Darwinian jungle of Victorian football, the club would have to cast off its suffocating Kentish outback for pastures new. The relocation to Highbury in North London saw the club begin to shed its rough and ready origins. With superior transport links to the West End, the club could draw in support from Holborn, King's Cross, Hackney and Finchley. When the great pioneer Herbert Chapman began to yield his guiding hand over Highbury's upgrade in the 1930s, he was able to further alter the genome of the match-day crowd.

With the erection of the palatial East Stand in 1936, replete with Marble Halls, club restaurant, oak panelled offices and hat doffing commissionaire greeting entrants, the club were able to attract the great and good of London's social coterie to match days. In the 1930s, Hollywood actor Buster Keaton was a regular in Arsenal's corporate hospitality. The upper tier of the East Stand was even embossed with a concrete rendering of a theatre curtain. The allusions to class and stature were clear and Highbury threw its doors open to the upper middle-classes. Such luxury would quite literally have been a pipe dream to the munitions men who stood on the Southern Outfall Sewer pipe to watch Woolwich Arsenal games some 40 years earlier.

Following the conclusion of the Second World War and the resumption of League Football in the late 40s, fans flocked back to the Highbury terraces to find further change afoot. The crowd canvas was beginning to fleck with colour. As Islington began to experience an influx of Italian and Greek Cypriot communities setting up local businesses, so the Mediterranean influence began to embroider itself into the match-day experience. Philippos Anastasi is a Greek Cypriot immigrant who moved to Redbridge in 1955 and immediately became a regular at Highbury. He points to the inexpensiveness of watching Arsenal in the 1950's as a main reason that he began attending games. "I could go and see a relatively successful team which wasn't too far away from me and didn't cost a lot of money." Philippos also reasons that, despite the generally conservative outlook of 1950s Britain, Highbury was always welcoming to other cultures. "I never once encountered any hostility. Even though my English wasn't very good, I always felt welcome at Highbury. The enemy was always the opposition."

Singing on the terraces was a rare convention in the early 50's and anathema to the stiff-upper-lipped Englishmen. But with the more expressive Latin and Hellenic influence at Highbury, the popular Arsenal ditty "Anchors Aweigh" began to make itself heard with greater gusto. Philippos concurs that the presence of more effusive cultures began to help the vocal element of the Highbury support along. "I would go with my friend Savvos and we would cheer the loudest, even though we didn't know what we were saying half the time! I think the passion and the love those supporters brought to the game really added to the atmosphere."

By the 1960's, the custom of terrace chanting had become ingratiated into the match-day experience. With the screaming hysteria of Beatlemania, the copycat opportunities offered by Match of the Day, and the anthemic pop music proffered by the likes of the Stones and the Who, football crowds became more rumbustious. Highbury was no different and the terraces began to take on a more sinister edge as wide-eyed, amphetamine fuelled gangs such as the Islington Angels and the Finchley Boys began to roam the North Bank. The 60's saw crowds drop at Highbury. The voracious appetite for football in the immediate post war era was not quite as conspicuous, but also largely because Arsenal were marooned in mid-table for much of the decade. Highbury's more middle-aged clientele had been reared on the unprecedented success of the Chapman and Allison pre war era. They were beginning to lose hope that Arsenal could ever recapture those former glories. The Highbury crowd began to take on a much more youthful complexion.

Siphoned away on the North Bank and Clock End, away from the disapproving eyes of their parents, teenage boys were altering the fabric of the famous old ground; sometimes literally. Prior to the baby boomers, dark suits, cloth caps and rolled up cigarettes were the conservative uniform of the match going supporter. But by the mid-60's, the wallflower element that had become part of youth culture was infiltrating football grounds too. Red and white rosettes and scarves were now de rigueur. Cherry red Doctor Martens, rolled up Levi's and suede head haircuts were making their way onto the terrace catwalk. Fashion at the time dictated that red and white scarves were tied around wrists to complete the look.

The birth of rock 'n' roll in the 1950's fastened carefully groomed image to youth culture. With cultural icons such as James Dean and the landmark movie 'Rebel Without A Cause' and with British gangs such as mods and rockers identifying their allegiance through uniform, British terraces were soon peacocking to the whims of the fashions; and with it a more sinister edge emerged. With improvements in public transport, away support became more commonplace inside Highbury. Typically, travellers from Liverpool, Manchester or the Midlands poured in from Arsenal station at around 2.55pm and congregated on the nearby Clock End. Tension was starting to creep inside the walls of the famous old stadium and stadiums around the country. Coins with serrated edges were tossed between rival supporters, bloody retributions were exacted. Though Highbury was one of the more moderate grounds in this climate, it was clear to see it was no longer a place where working class men went to drink, smoke and swear. The release valve people would find by attending matches at Highbury was beginning to manifest itself more aggressively.

In the early 1970's, the Arsenal crowd was about to find its first idol, reared as he was against this backdrop of 1960s Highbury. He would become an on-pitch avatar for the hopes and dreams for the fans; a young man who had attended games in drainpipe jeans and Doc Martens. Charlie George was probably the first Arsenal player who visibly reflected the voguish palpitations of the Highbury crowd. When George made his debut in 1969, his aesthetic typified those of the teenage rabble watching him from the North Bank; the cropped, suede-head haircut, the quiet air of moody nonchalance. By the early 70's, Charlie had let the tight crop unfurl into a flowing mane. The supporters followed suit – though whether it was George, or bands such as Led Zeppelin and Pink Floyd that influenced this follicular phenomenon is open to debate. But George also brought an air of disaffected, inner-city aggression onto the pitch with him. In an interview with the Daily Express in December 1970, George laconically summed up his outlook towards less-forgiving opponents. "If anyone thumps me, I just nut them." With his cocky cockney swagger and Islington upbringing, George readily became an icon because the supporters identified with him. Had they been on the pitch, they'd have played like George did. There was a common expression at the time, that George had hopped the North Bank fence and onto the pitch. His connection with the supporters represented a sea change for the Highbury crowd. Though the team of the 30's were revered and accessible; they were looked upon almost as apotheoses: untouchable figures of athletic perfection. George's lank hair and cocksure snarl represented a severance with the polished Brylcreem boys of yore. George was Arsenal's first rock star.

Charlie George would leave the club contentiously in 1975. But the umbilical relationship between the stands and the pitch remained. The area of Finsbury Park has long hosted a burgeoning Irish community. As such, Arsenal always had a sprinkling of green in its fan base, but by the late 1970's, the stands began to slowly reverberate to the twang of Irish accents. This was precipitated in part by the fact that, under Ulsterman Terry Neill, the Gunners earned themselves the press nickname 'London Irish'. With the likes of David O'Leary, John Devine and Frank Stapleton making up the Republic contingent, whilst Pat Jennings, Sammy Nelson and captain Pat Rice made up the Northern Irish quota.

The shining beacon from the Emerald Isles next invading Highbury was a young genius by the name Liam Brady, Highbury's next terrace legend. Brady was a distinctively Irish sort of hero. Articulate and outspoken, he played like a scruffy artiste. The constantly un-tucked shirt and half-mast socks provided a striking contrast to the gracile quality of his play. If George was Jagger – snarling and pouting – Brady was Richards: perhaps slightly more introspective, but no less devastating. The Irish theme was quick to make its mark on the club. It was around this time that the Irish folk anthem 'Bejesus Said Paddy' began to resonate around the stadium. The club played to the theme too, when they released 'Super Arsenal', an adaptation of an old Irish folk song, as their 1979 F.A. Cup Final chart entry.

Brian Magorrian is an Arsenal season ticket holder who was born and raised in Belfast in the 1970's. Brian contends that, whilst the Irish population of North London may have been flocking towards Highbury, the actual impact of the 'London Irish' team was not as culturally significant in Northern Ireland at least. "Arsenal were always popular in Northern Ireland and the Irish connection might have strengthened that. But we were still well outnumbered by Manchester United, Liverpool, Celtic and Rangers. At the time, Arsenal were the third most popular English club in Northern Ireland and I think that's still the case."

Of course, the concoction of Northern and Southern Irish players at Arsenal led to some mischief making in the press. Stories were rife of dressing room discord, with differences in religion and politics at the epicentre of the conflict. Terry Neill and the players have always laughed off such stories. This seems to chime with Brian's experiences in Belfast, "I don't remember any tension related to that. It certainly never affected me and I could always happily wear an Arsenal badge in Belfast."

The adoption of cult heroes such as Brady and George began to demonstrate the sociological currency players could hold with supporters. Through the 1980's, at a time when racial tension was at a threshold in British football grounds, Arsenal used notably more black players than most other teams. The likes of Viv Anderson, Chris Whyte, Raphael Meade, Paul Davis and the incomparable David Rocastle were regular fixtures in the side. Holloway and Finsbury Park have long boasted proud African and Caribbean communities. Once again, this began to reflect in the Highbury melting pot. At last known count, around 9% of Arsenal's season ticket holders were non-white. Moving into the early 90's when players like Kevin Campbell and Ian Wright were mainstays of the team, bringing contemporary reggae dances into their choreographed goal celebrations, a generation of young black men flocked to Highbury. Arsenal's corner of North London has long seen migrant communities lay their roots into its soil – which has mirrored in the support. However, the sense of identity with the club's multicultural playing staff is likely to have had as magnetic an influence.

Though not raised in North London, Ian Wright and David Rocastle (both from Lewisham) were gracing the side come the early 90's. They were young, working-class black men raised on inner-city council estates, not dissimilar to the ones that populate the Islington horizon. Much in the same vein as Charlie George had won the affections of the North Bank with his devil-may-care demeanour; Ian Wright likewise became a conduit between the stands and the pitch. His expressiveness, his distaste for authority, and his brusqueness could all be seen to have their roots in inner-city culture. Wright was loved by Arsenal fans, regardless of creed, because he played with his heart on his sleeve.

I was between primary and secondary school in South East London when Wright was in his prime at Arsenal. To my recollection, nearly all of the black pupils at my school were Arsenal supporters and Wright was a big reason for that. He exuded charisma in a way that was rooted into hip-hop culture. The swagger and self-belief remained a constant, even when he found disillusion with the establishment. Nike cleverly exploited that connection with their early 90's advertisement depicting Wright's goal scoring feats against the strains of A Tribe Called Quest's 'Can I Kick It'.

With the arrival of Sky television and Internet technology, which allows games to be streamed all over the world, the relationship between a club's fans and its community is no longer as pronounced. Somebody in rural New Zealand is as likely to watch an Arsenal match in real time as somebody in N5. So whilst the supporter net has become wider and more diverse, these changes are more a wider symptom of the global village we inhabit. The reason Arsenal were greeted by thousands of excited Malaysian and Chinese fans in the summer of 2011is less to do with the fluctuations of the Islington community and more a result of instant technology and marketing.

It would of course be incorrect to paint Arsenal as having always been a puritanical liberal utopia entirely free of prejudice. The prevalence of the Jewish hamlet in Tottenham means that unfavourable anti-Semitic language has been commonly heard on Arsenal's terraces through the years. Aggressively anti-Semitic songs are heard rarely in this day and age at Arsenal, yet use of the term "Yids" in reference to Tottenham fans is still part of the everyday lexicon at matches. However, in its 125 years, the club's support base has vacillated. Different cultures have become implanted into the club's identity. Maybe I am looking generously through the prism of club bias, but Arsenal genuinely strikes me as a club with a more dynamic tapestry behind it. The club's status as that of liberal progressive institution has been furthered passionately by Arsene Wenger. Lest we forget, Mr Wenger is the only manager ever to name eleven different nationalities in his team for a Champions' League fixture against Hamburg in September 2006.

The club and the supporters that breathe life into it have come a long way, baby. From the dirt underneath the fingernails of the munitions workers, who hauled the club up by its bootstraps through the jungle of Victorian football. The club became a migrant in its own right a touch under a century ago. The club's nomadic history, from the Manor Ground to Highbury, and latterly to the Emirates, is a fitting indication indeed of the array of cultures that have enriched the institution ever since.

Tim Stillman has been blogging on all matters Arsenal since 2006. Tim has been shunning human relationships to follow Arsenal over land and sea since childhood.

4

DENNIS

PAOLO BANDINI

It takes something quite special to give Ian Wright an inferiority complex. "We are not worthy," hailed Wright, leading his team-mates in a deferential bow, as Dennis Bergkamp attempted an introductory speech at his first Arsenal training session back in July 1995. The tone may have been light-hearted but the sentiment was sincere. Never before had London Colney played host to a talent quite like this one.

Dennis Bergkamp. *The* Dennis Bergkamp: blond-haired, blue-eyed star of the Dutch national side, joint-top scorer at Euro 92 and artful annihilator of England's World Cup 1994 qualification hopes. A graduate of the Ajax youth academy who had been mentored by Johan Cruyff and topped the Dutch scoring charts for three years running and twice finished in the top three of the Ballon d'Or voting. A player who had joined Serie A's Internazionale two years earlier for an eye-watering £12m – just £1m shy of the then world transfer record.

If Arsenal was hardly a footballing backwater – a club just one year removed from Cup Winners' Cup triumph and two from a domestic cup double – then it is also fair to say that they had never before shopped in this aisle of the transfer market. The £7.5m paid to Inter represented a trebling of the club's record outlay. Indeed, for the briefest of moments it was a British transfer record – before Liverpool completed their £8.5m purchase of Stan Collymore from Nottingham Forest. Furthermore Arsenal had shattered their wage structure with a package worth £25,000 per week, prompting the chairman Peter Hill-Wood to decry his own club's spending as "absolutely mad". He also offered a justification, however. "We have got better value for money than some of the big transfers of late," he noted. "This player we have bought is truly world-class."

That, in itself, seemed an alien notion at a time when every Premier League squad remained overwhelmingly British and Irish. Although there were a number of talented and productive foreign players throughout the division, English clubs did not yet boast the resources to compete financially with the continent's richest sides. Arsenal's own foreign legion extended to Glenn Helder and John Jensen. The great players who did arrive from abroad often came with a caveat. Eric Cantona moved to England only after becoming so enraged by decisions handed down by the French Football Federation that he briefly toyed with retirement. Jurgen Klinsmann's one-year stay at Tottenham had concluded with the club's chairman Alan Sugar railing against "Carlos Kickaball" foreigners exploiting British generosity to make a quick buck.

Bergkamp also came with red flags against his name. His time at Inter had not been a happy one, marked by just 11 goals in 52 Serie A outings, and a difficult relationship with the Italian press. Uncomfortable with the intensity of media spotlight in Italy, Bergkamp was labelled aloof for declining interviews, and cold for not being more verbose when he did give them. Even several years after his move to England, the newspaper La Repubblica protested that dealing with Bergkamp had been "like talking to a cash machine." In the absence of direct quotes from the player, the speculation had been relentless. "For a while when he was at Inter, Bergkamp had a high Rockabilly quiff – very blond – but then at a certain point he decided to cut it short," recalls David Winner, author of *Brilliant Orange: the neurotic genius of Dutch football*. "So then this story shows up in Gazzetta dello Sport saying his hair was falling out because of the stress."

But if said haircut also contributed to Bergkamp acquiring the nickname Beavis – on account of his perceived likeness to MTV's chortling cartoon teenager – then it was Moratti who behaved like a Butthead. In persuading the Dutchman to join in the first place from Ajax, the Inter president promised his new signing that the team would be built around him – with an attacking formation designed to make the most of his talents. The experiment lasted barely a month, abandoned after a poor start to the season and long forgotten by the time of his departure – two managerial changes later.

The very words with which Moratti damned Bergkamp after completing his sale betrayed how Inter had misunderstood the Dutchman's genius. "Arsenal will be lucky if Bergkamp scores 10 goals this year," crowed the Inter owner. From a statistical perspective he wasn't that far wide of the mark, Bergkamp concluded the 1995-96 campaign with a modest 11 from 33 league games. The difference at Arsenal was that his contribution was measured by far more than just how many times he hit the net.

Where Inter had too often used Bergkamp as a lone striker, at Arsenal Ian Wright was only too happy to shoulder the goal-scoring burden – leaving the Dutchman free to take up deeper positions, to focus his energies at times on creating opportunities instead of finishing them. He provided eight league assists in his first season, a figure that would rise steadily over the following three campaigns. Even Bergkamp would be surprised by the enjoyment he derived from his new role. "It [Putting a player through on goal] gave me so much pleasure, like solving a puzzle," he told Winner in a recent interview for football magazine The Blizzard. "Scoring goals is, of course, up there.

It is known. It is like nothing else. But for me, in the end, giving the assist got closer and closer to that feeling."

Which is not to say that goals were unimportant, and especially at the outset there was a pressure to justify such a high price tag. "Dennis Bergkamp is a £7.5million striker playing like someone who cost 75p," scoffed Mark Lawrenson in the Mirror in late September, after the Dutchman failed to score in any of his first six league games for the club. "Hartle-Fool" read a headline in the same paper when Bergkamp failed to get off the mark in a League Cup game against third division Hartlepool United. And yet, when Bergkamp's first goals for Arsenal finally arrived – a few days later in a 4-2 win over Southampton at Highbury – they seemed sufficient to dispel such doubts at a stroke. If the opener, a cushioned volley back across goal from Helder's looping, slow-motion, cross, demonstrated impeccable technique, then the second was of such quality that Bergkamp immediately declared it to be "in my top three of all time." Receiving a pass from Tony Adams inside the Southampton half, Bergkamp glided forward 20 yards, cut sharply to the right to shed his marker then arrowed a shot straight into the top corner while yellow-striped defenders buzzed around him like angry, impotent bees. It was the culmination of a performance of the highest order, one that began in the very first minute, when Bergkamp picked out Lee Dixon with a breath-taking cross-field pass that almost led to a Paul Merson opener. The drought over, reporters turned their attention elsewhere.

Unlike their Italian counterparts, English tabloid reporters were interested in the private lives only of those players
who liked to live fast. Bergkamp, more than one newspaper
noted approvingly, was a quiet soul who enjoyed tending to
his garden. Little wonder – one of his lowest moments for
in Milan had arrived when reporters resorted to interview-
ing his gardener, who had cheerily portrayed Bergkamp as
a hopeless case who spent every waking minute in front of
a telly.

Yet the Bergkamp who showed up in north London was
anything but a social misfit. By his own admission, the
Dutchman was surprised by the English drinking culture
and did not himself partake, but he respected his team-
mates' right to make their own decisions. "The funny thing
is you never noticed it in training because they were so
strong and they always gave 100 per cent," he would later
note. His teammates, meanwhile, would quickly discover
that behind the Iceman façade lay a mischievous sense of
humour. "He had this big, toothy grin. He was the kind of
person who just loved football, and he expressed himself
best in a football club," recalls Martin Keown. "He enjoyed
a practical joke. If your gear was hanging up from the ceiling you'd pretty well know it was Dennis who put it there."

For Bergkamp, it had been a life-long dream to play in
England – an ambition formed during so many childhood
pilgrimages to watch matches there with his father. Wim
Bergkamp was unashamedly fixated with the British game,

so much so that he had sought to name his son after Denis
Law, only for a fussy civil servant to insist on the insertion
of a second 'n'. Dennis himself idolised Glenn Hoddle,
though he has often stressed that this did not make him
a supporter of Tottenham. Arsenal at the time might not
have seemed the most obvious fit for a player motivated to
escape the defensive clutches of Serie A, committed as they
were, in the latter days of George Graham's reign, to what
Winner eloquently terms a "grubby English catenaccio".

Graham himself had been sacked, of course, for accepting illegal payments from the agent Rune Hauge, but this
was still a team built to defend first and foremost, and there
was no guarantee of a transformation in approach under his
successor Bruce Rioch. But for all that Bergkamp spoke in
his early interviews of excitement at the attacking nature of
Premier League football and the joy of playing alongside a
goalscorer like Wright; he also admired the old-fashioned
toughness of Arsenal's back line. In his third pre-season
fixture for Arsenal, against his former club Inter, a torrent
of abuse from his former team-mate Nicola Berti was cut
short when Tony Adams stepped up to the Inter midfielder.
"Our English defenders put the spirit in the team, which the
Europeans lacked," Bergkamp would reflect in an interview
with the magazine FourFourTwo many years later. "They
would say, 'Get stuck in!' and all sorts of other phrases. I
loved it, especially: 'How much do you want it?' I thought
about it. It stuck with me. Do you really want it more than

the opponent? How much are you prepared to give? How much time do you want to put in to become better?"

Certainly Bergkamp was not afraid of putting in the hours. On the Monday after a match he could regularly be found lining up free kicks on an empty training field long after the main session had ended. And for as long as his team-mates did hang around, he was helping them develop too – communicating his own ideas as well as techniques he had picked up at Ajax, where the academy required its students to train in every outfield position over the course of their development. "For me as a defender it was a chance to pit your wits every day against a genius," says Keown. "But he made it easy to play with him as well. He pulled me over in training one day and said 'we're going to do opposite movements.' So if he stepped forwards he wanted the ball behind the opponent, and vice-versa. Wrighty, for instance, might run 10 yards in the direction opposite to where he would want it, and then step out. But with Dennis it would be literally just the drop of a shoulder, little signals that made it very easy to find him."

From 12th place finishers the season before, Arsenal finished Bergkamp's first campaign in fifth – the Dutchman scoring the winning goal against Bolton to secure a UEFA Cup berth after his fellow summer signing, David Platt, brought the team back from a goal down. At the time it felt like a significant achievement in its own right, but the real revolution was just around the corner. Late in the ensuing summer, Rioch would be sacked and replaced by Arsène Wenger. Bergkamp had been fond of Rioch, describing his departure as "a big blow to me," yet he soon identified in Wenger a kindred spirit. The forward who once mused "I suppose I'm not that interested in scoring ugly goals," finally had a manager who recognised the value of the aesthetic, as well as the end product. They also had shared ideas about the requirements of being a professional. While Wenger's tough dietary regimen came as a shock to the system for some, in Bergkamp's case he was preaching to the converted. The Dutchman had previously always declined the food served London Colney but now was first in line. If Wenger's arrival marked the start of what would be termed a French revolution for Arsenal then it would be another year before they would be ready to overthrow the ruling elite. After a third-place finish in 1996-97 Arsenal began the following campaign with a 12-game unbeaten run with Bergkamp on blistering form. His hat-trick in a 3-3 draw against Leicester at Filbert Street, famously, would claim first, second and third place in Match of the Day's Goal of the Month competition. While the first two strikes had been impressive – an inch-perfect effort from the corner of the area that arced over a horde of players and into the top corner, then a delicate finish to complete a sweeping counter-attack – the third was of a different order. Racing into the area to meet a chipped pass from David Platt, Bergkamp cushioned the ball with first his right, and then, without letting it touch the ground, his left, wrong-footing his marker Matt Elliot in the process as he shifted the ball back across his body before side-footing it across the keeper into the net. It remains Bergkamp's personal favourite from his time at Arsenal – ahead even of the goal he would score against Newcastle in 2002, caressing the ball around Nikos Dabizas before spinning around the defender in the opposite direction to slot the ball home. The latter would go on to be voted by fans as Arsenal's greatest goal of all time, but for Bergkamp the strike against Leicester was more "pure". Dabizas, he reasoned, could have stopped him had he taken a step back at the crucial moment. Elliot never had a chance.

But if Bergkamp was showing his brilliant best at this stage then he was also showing his petulant worst. By the 11th game of the season he had already collected his fifth booking and with it an automatic ban. During his absence, Arsenal lost their first game of the campaign – a 3-0 rout at Derby, sparking a sequence of four defeats in six league matches. Having learnt the game playing out on tarmacked streets, it was perhaps no surprise that Bergkamp had never really worked out how to tackle. Nor, indeed, quite come to terms with the idea of others tackling him. Over the course of 1997-98 he would pick up nine yellow cards and one red, earned after introducing his elbow to Steve Lomas's face during an FA Cup replay in March. It was the second of four dismissals he would collect in his Arsenal career. The vicious streak was not just restricted to matches.

"He certainly knew how to look after himself," says Nigel Winterburn. "I remember playing an eight v eight game, and I was playing at the back with Steve Bould. Steve had kicked Dennis a couple of times and you could see Dennis getting wild. I came in behind to mark him on the next occasion and ended up with the fattest lip you'd ever seen."

Yet perhaps such an edge was exactly what was required to compete for titles and after a mid-season lull Bergkamp continued to be the key protagonist of a campaign that finished with not only a first league title in seven years, but the FA Cup to boot. By the end of the campaign, Bergkamp would become the first man from outside Britain to win both the Football Writers' Association and the Professional Footballers' Association's player of the year awards in the same season. Not that Bergkamp especially wanted to be thought of as a foreigner. His successes in the English game, allied to those of players brought in by Wenger, would prove the precursor to a massive influx of foreign players into the Premier League, as teams became aware of the value to be had abroad and players of the growing wages on offer in England as television revenues grew. Yet Bergkamp was as wary as Sugar had been of Carlos Kickaball. "I often feel quite protective of the league like a child who doesn't want to share with others," he noted in 2003. "I've often looked at other foreign players and thought, 'You have no right to be here. I've put a lot of work in to prove that foreigners can make a difference in England, so why are you coming here to ruin that?'"

Bergkamp promised when he arrived that he was here for the long haul and he was as good as his word. Over 11 years he would stay committed to Arsenal, faithful even in the dark days when it seemed their devotion to him might be wavering. Days such as the one, shortly after he declared his international retirement in order to concentrate on his club football, when Wenger said that his spot, too, would be subject to squad rotation. That was in 2000, a year further darkened by a combination of Achilles injury and self-doubt; yet a season later there was Bergkamp, pulling the strings once again as Arsenal repeated their double triumph of four years previous. He would also be there to lift the FA Cup in 2003 and 2005, as well as to claim a further Premier League winner's medal in-between. In the end he would be with the club until 2006, retiring an Arsenal player at the ripe old age of 37. If there was to be one regret, in the end, it was that he never managed to lift a European trophy with Arsenal. He had been withdrawn after 75 minutes of the lost UEFA Cup final against Galatasaray in 2000, and never made it off the bench when Arsenal were beaten 2-1 by Barcelona in the Champions League showpiece six years later.

Few fans have not wondered at some point whether things might have been different had Bergkamp not missed, or at least been hindered, in so many European away fixtures by his refusal to fly. Certainly it was a favoured topic for the British press for a time with newspapers variously drawing up schedules to get the player to matches and one or two reporters even attempting to replicate his routes themselves (in one newspaper's case, even taking a cardboard cut-out of the player along for the ride). But for all the words expended on the topic it may have been something of a red herring. It was, after all, Arsenal's home form in Europe that had done more than anything to undermine their prospects during Bergkamp's best years at the club. In both 1996-97 and 1997-98 the club exited the UEFA Cup at the first hurdle after failing to win the home leg of their first round fixtures, while over the following two seasons they would win just two of six home Champions League fixtures following an ill-advised plan to relocate to Wembley for European fixtures. Besides, in the final analysis, judging Bergkamp's career on trophies at all feels like it might be missing the point. After all, ask a fan, or even a team-mate for their fondest of memory of the Dutchman and they do not talk of trophies but of individual goals, assists, or even just a touch that made the heart sing. They will tell you about the Leicester hat-trick, the gleeful hand-over-mouth celebration after scoring against Sunderland or the absurd game of cat and mouse with three Juventus defenders in December 2001 – capped with an outrageous outside-of-the-boot, chipped, through-ball for Freddie Ljungberg that left one Dutch commentator bellowing "Harry Potter! Harry Potter!" into the night sky. Or indeed the act of wizardry against Argentina at the 1998 World Cup which rendered another TV announcer incapable of doing anything but screaming the player's name over and over.

The reality is that Bergkamp was not always the most effective player on the pitch – indeed, there were lengthy spells at Arsenal when he felt like the precise opposite: an anonymous, sulking presence more likely to chop down an opponent than slice open a defence. When the journalist Henk Spaan published his book Top 100: The Best Dutch Footballers of the Century in 1998, he placed Bergkamp a lowly 12th. Bergkamp, admittedly, had a good few years left in him at that time, but as many people might still agree with that verdict now as did then; others would make him an emphatic first. You would, as Simon Kuper wrote in the Financial Times, "never want Bergkamp playing for your life," but for a spell he just might have been the player you most wished to see play before you died.

"I used to say the same about Liam Brady back when I was a season ticket holder," says former Arsenal vice-chairman David Dein. "He was worth the entrance money alone."

Even if only to find out what sort of man could have that effect on Wrighty.

Paolo Bandini writes for the Guardian, plus one or two others. He once made Ian Wright cry with laughter by bringing a 'Keown for England' sign to an away game against Wimbledon

5

HIGHBURY V EMIRATES

JIM HARYOTT

You'd think there would be no comparison. An elderly, compact and – whisper it quietly – rather dog-eared stadium pits itself head-to-head against a state-of-the-art, squidgy-seated, curvaceous megabowl of an arena. The latter, a docked spacecraft bristling with steel and concrete; boasting 22,000 more seats than its predecessor and generally speaking, infinitely more suitable to football in the modern era, should win the contest hands down.

And yet, and yet... my own memories of Highbury grow fonder over time.

It's not that I don't like The Emirates – or if you'd prefer, because it probably won't be a middle-eastern airline forever – Ashburton Grove. For the most part, I love it. I watched it grow, via a webcam, like an expectant father. From the very first moment I set foot inside it (a 1-1 home draw against Villa, its first competitive match) I was taken aback by its scale. Sure, repeated visits have dampened the novelty somewhat, but even now, during a mid-game lull or when we find ourselves 1-0 down after 15 minutes, I crane my neck and admire the beauty of its wavy lines and mammoth roof struts (are they struts? I have no idea – but let's call them struts for the sake of argument). It's a stunning football stadium. The pitch is vast and in a permanent state of perfection. The seats are wide enough for all girths and soft enough for the boniest of behinds. There are urinals and toilets aplenty, into which the club pipes in an incredibly realistic waft of tobacco smoke every half time to remind us all of the olden days (at least I think that's what's going on). You can hear actual words coming out of the tannoy. It's the best-looking club-ground in England, though I might, of course, be blinkered. It holds over 60,000 fans, which is more than Highbury had held for a very long time indeed, and rather amazingly, it's almost always full, or at least sold out.

But perhaps best of all, it's a mere Delap throw from the old place. For many people, perhaps most people, the routines and tics picked up through years of trudging to Highbury remain. The same tube station, the same pub, the same burger stand. It's a world away from Highbury and yet it's strangely familiar. Even now, I shudder to think how things might have been had it not panned out the way it did. The club found enough inner-city land practically next door. How unlikely is that? It secured an absurd amount of money at favourable rates – how many clubs could do that now? Look at the desperation of other clubs in London to secure new premises, and marvel at what our club did, and how they did it, ten years before others started fretting about their own futures. Sharing Wembley? It would have ripped the heart out of the club. No: the move to the Emirates was the best possible outcome to an intractable problem. How do you let more fans in, and how do you make more match-day money, at a ground hemmed in by Victorian terraces?

And yet you only have to look at some of the work that's gone on at the Emirates since it opened to realise that there are some things the march of progress has trampled on. Some of it unintentional, and some of it unavoidable, true; but all the same, it's happened. Since 2006, there have been repeated, mostly admirable attempts to 'Arsenalise' the Emirates. It's a word I hate but it implies the new place doesn't yet really feel like 'home', and there's a definite element of truth in that. Gone are the concrete facades of the tiers, replaced by a chronology of trophy-winning years – still resolutely blank after 2005, but you can hardly blame that on the stadium, can you? In have come murals, and pictures, and other memorabilia to make the new place feel a bit more, well, like the old place. The ends have been renamed North Bank, Clock End, East Stand and West Stand (as they should have been from the word go). The famous clock – or at least, a replica of it – once again hangs above the Clock End. It feels more like home than it ever has, but there's only so much that can be done to speed up its assimilation into the hearts of those of us who knew and loved Highbury. In reality, the only things that will make that happen are memorable matches and trophies. But mostly I suspect it's the passage of time that will do the best job.

There are of course downsides, not all of which can be attributed solely to Arsenal moving ground. The Emirates is as much about making money as it is about providing an arena for football – it's a hundred times brasher than Highbury was. The seats are now among the most expensive in the country, and indeed in Europe. Whole swathes of the ground are given over to corporate entertainment. The food and drink – outsourced – is overpriced. Gone are the "Peeeeannnnuts!" at 20p a bag. Now we have 'meal-deals' costing the best part of a tenner. Rolling up at the Highbury turnstiles in the 1980s cost about £5. Now you'll get no change out of about £40, and football ticketing these days dictates that there's very little room to spontaneously roll up to a game anymore, without a ticket, and expect to get in.

At Highbury, the Gunners Shop by the Clock End on Avenell Road was so small it operated a one-in, one-out policy on match-days. There were scarves and rattles and ashtrays and *Charlie Is My Darling* scarves, but it all squeezed into a room about the size of a corner shop. The Emirates now oozes merchandising outlets – there are now even retail kiosks in the concourse areas, just in case you want to tip-toe out of the game eight minutes before half-time rather than a mere three minutes before half-time, which is the current norm. Football now and football then – everywhere, probably, but at Arsenal, certainly – are worlds apart.

An additional 22,000 fans, rather than creating a better atmosphere, have diluted it. It seems impossible, but it's true. Again, that's not all down to the move. It's been happening at Arsenal since the terraces were replaced by seats, but the move to the new ground did seem to accelerate it. Now we have singing areas (a fantastic idea) and piped crowd noise, flags, balloons and so on (you can't blame them for trying) – all to generate something that used to come naturally at Highbury. People arrive increasingly late and leave early, or they don't turn up at all, despite having bought a ticket. It seems odd to me to travel long distances only to miss ten or twenty percent of what you came to see, but there you go. It happened at Highbury, for sure, but it didn't happen so much.

But maybe we tend to look back at the 'good old days' when really, perhaps they weren't that good after all. In the 70's and 80's, the football at Highbury was often functional at best; hooliganism was more prevalent – though Arsenal to their credit always refused to fence fans in – and to get

20,000 for a league game was not abnormal. The facilities at Highbury, compared to those you get now, were lacking, though they were nothing unusual then and an awful lot better than some grounds. Since the Taylor Report, and the Premier League, football changed irrevocably and in the end, it signalled the death knell for Highbury and its old-world comforts. A capacity that used to be about 57,000 (if everyone got a bit cosy) shrank to 38,000 in about seven years. Rather ironically, the huge reduction in capacity began to happen at a time of re-emergence on the pitch. George Graham's young, vibrant side of the late 1980's threw Arsenal's lethargy off, winning two titles and four cups, before the baton was picked up by Wenger. Suddenly, thousands more people wanted to come, but couldn't.

Some things though have not been redefined in my mind over the passage of time. They are plain fact. Highbury was definitely more affordable and the atmosphere there was definitely better. Turning up an hour early to a big game in the 80's not only guaranteed several throaty renditions of the best songs, but if you didn't get there in good time you'd either not get in at all, or you'd be squeezed out of the action on the sides of the terraces. My first season ticket, in 1994, cost around £200. Now, the equivalent seat costs £1,000.

I think back to the kinds of atmospheres generated on big nights at Highbury and compare them with those we have had to date at the Emirates; there is no comparison. The 2-1 defeat of Barcelona in February 2011 comes nearest: the place was a crackling cauldron and had all the ingredients for a bubbling atmosphere: a quick-fire comeback against arguably the best club side of this generation. But I can think of many better memories at Highbury. I'll never forget the opening day of the season in 1987, against Liverpool, when over 54,000 squeezed into Highbury. Gates closed an hour before the game. People ended up sitting on the roof of the North Bank. The terrace was one vast, bubbling, ebbing and flowing mass of humanity. The noise was relentless and we sang ourselves hoarse. I'm not sure we will ever see the likes of that again at the Emirates.

And then there are the titles and the title run-ins. It's hard to define exactly why, but the 'We're going to win the league' moments are hard to beat; those specific points in a season when the whole stadium – as one – realises the title is within grasp, and starts to sing. The surge of expectancy, of excitement, coupled with an underlying, gnawing fear of failure; it grabs the pit of your stomach. It's magical. We've not had that at the Emirates. As for the titles themselves: Adams dancing through Everton's defence to pick up Bould's through pass will take some beating. Gathering below the home dressing room, serenading players in 1991, 1998, 2002, 2004. Those are the kinds of things that add to the aura of a ground, to its history. You can't pluck them from a marketing manual.

With regard to Highbury itself, well it might have been long in the tooth in its latter years, but it was still one of the most elegant grounds in the country. Archibald Leitch's listed Art Deco stands, the bust of Herbert Chapman, the Marble Halls, the commissionaire stationed outside the entrance to the East Stand; it stank of history, and class seeped from its every pore. The first time I went there, one Saturday at 3 o'clock in December 1985 (back then it was of course almost always Saturday at 3 o'clock) is partly vivid and partly completely forgotten. As, if I am honest, is my memory of most games since. Above all else I remember emerging into the sun of West Stand Upper tier, peering down at this impossibly high, impossibly large and impossibly noisy cathedral of football. I was awestruck. I have a vague memory of Niall Quinn scoring on his debut, and of Charlie Nicholas getting one too, but details of the goals themselves, and most other memories of the day, have retreated into the recesses of my mind. For years, I could recall the exact attendance, but at some point in the intervening decades I have forgotten the last three digits. It was 35 thousand and something. That's age for you.

Oddly, but this could again be an age thing, I have fewer crystal clear memories of my first trip to the Emirates than I do of my first visit to Highbury. I have a feeling I spent most of my time craning my neck at its architectural glory. I do remember we equalised to ensure its debut didn't go too flat... but that's about it. I could only guess at the line-up now (Justin Hoyte started – who knew?). In fact, I have had to look back at my blog entry for more prompting.

Turns out it was Walcott's debut, we were 'guilty of over-elaboration' and the queues for beer were frustratingly long. Glad all that's been fixed these last five years, eh…?

Thinking back to Highbury though, some of my own little favourite bits make no real sense at all: The 'JVC and Arsenal: A Perfect Match' signs on the side of the East and West stands. The precipitous walk up to the North Bank from Gillespie Road, manned turnstiles, complete with piles of match-day stubs; the programme seller's cupboard under the stairs. If pushed, I would say my favourite thing about the Emirates is the view as you walk up to it on a dark week-day evening, lit up, buzzing, grand and magnificent.

I was weaned on Highbury for twenty-years, and the Emirates has only been with us for five, so it's perhaps no great surprise that I look back at the old place more fondly than I do the new. My first visit, those seminal early years in any fan's life, all took place at Highbury. Will the latest generation of fans – those who have been coming to the Arsenal only since 2006, or who have been watching Arsenal somewhere across the globe only since then – have similar rose-tinted specs in 15 years? My son, whose first game came last season, a 2-1 home defeat by Aston Villa, already wants to go back, and back again, to the Emirates. So inevitably, they will. It's a wonderful stadium and it's the only place they have ever known.

Me? Well I'm afraid I'll be – if I'm not already – one of those old buggers who waxes on about the good old days at every opportunity. My love for Arsenal was forged at Highbury. The players I grew up on, whose careers I saw start and end, graced it; Seaman, Big Tone, Bouldy, Keown, Dicko, Nige, Paul Davis, Rocky, Steve Williams, The Merse, Michael Thomas, Alan Smith, Wrighty, Perry Groves, Petit, Vieira, Overmars, Henry, Le Bob, Dennis Bergkamp, Kaba Diawara and dozens besides. All those memories are Highbury memories.

I love the Emirates, and I doff my acrylic Kenny Sansom flat cap to its size, facilities and above all to its ambition, but in terms of memories it's just not there yet. How can it be? These things take time.

It's over to you, Emirates, to make up the deficit.

Jim Haryott started his blog, East Lower after Arsenal won the FA Cup in 2003 and has since enjoyed one glorious, unbeaten season, one jammy FA Cup, one oh-so-close European Cup final and, last but not least, six trophyless seasons. He's supported Arsenal since 1980, and to this day holds a grudge against Graham Rix for missing that penalty and making him cry

6

CONTINUED EVOLUTION

TOM CLARK

It's strange to me now, but being an Arsenal fan isn't something that always came naturally. When I was a small boy, I played football at school in both classes, and in the playground, but I wasn't that much of a fan of the game itself. I enjoyed it, sure, but I didn't play it with the same enthusiasm that I did rugby, or cricket, and I didn't really watch anything on the TV except the big games – FA Cup finals and the like – nor did I go to games. I didn't come from a footballing family. My parents didn't even have teams that they even nominally supported – and I can only remember one of my close friends specifically being a fan of a particular club: my best friend, in fact.

Robin, as we shall call him (for that was his name), did come from a footballing family. He had posters on his wall of his favourite players; both his father and his grandfather, who lived with them, were both season ticket holders. Robin and his older brother, Matt (also his name), went to games with their dad, and Matt played football in the school team. I even remember his mother wearing ribbons in her hair for a game. It may well even have been the 1987 cup final. In which Coventry City beat – yes, that's right – Tottenham Hotspur. My best friend Robin came from a family of die hard Spurs fans. The posters on his bedroom wall were of Hoddle, Waddle, and Ardiles.

I'm not a psychologist, and, it's been a quite a long while since I was a small boy, but I think it speaks volumes for the nature of small boy relationships that I ended up becoming a fan of my best friend's team's biggest rivals. That or I'm some kind of sociopath. I mean… what kind of kid does that? But, at that time, it simply didn't register as being possibly the most annoying and provocative thing I have ever done. Like many small boys, Robin and I were competitive. We competed over who had the best dad, whether the Atari or the Amiga was better than a BBC Micro (it totally wasn't), who was better friends with our mutual friend Greg; I clearly wanted another thing to compete over. Either way, I'm glad my friend Robin's family were Spurs fans. Things could well have turned out quite horribly had they been Arsenal fans.

As entertaining as that was, becoming an Arsenal fan wasn't only about diametrically opposing myself to the extended family of my so-called best friend. In truth, I was jealous.

The sense of belonging; of being part of a tribe, at one with culture, history, and identity are powerful ideas for a small boy. I mean, *obviously* I wasn't jealous enough to be part of Robin's particular poxy tribe, but the concept of belonging was appealing. I didn't rationalise and explain it to myself in quite the same way when I was ten, but there was definitely something that drew me in. So unlike many people, becoming an Arsenal fan was, for me, an active choice, and I chose it for that most healthy, positive, and constructive of reasons – the deep-rooted male need to compete with another male. To his credit, Robin took my massive insult to him and his family surprisingly well – it didn't really change anything between us and we remained friends.

I made friends with other Arsenal supporting kids, and it wasn't long before one of their families adopted me and I got to go to my first game at Highbury. The relationship was firmly established, and I was doing the things boys did: collecting Panini stickers, completing World Cup wall charts – pretending to be Arsenal players when we played football at school. I had posters on my bedroom wall. By the time 1989 and 1991 brought forth all their wonderful glories, I was thoroughly consumed. And then something rather unfortunate happened. My father was informed by his job that he had to relocate and was given the choice of either Singapore or Aberdeen. For one reason and another, he chose Aberdeen, which meant that we were moving from just outside London to the North-East of Scotland:

it might as well have been a million miles away. Aside from this being the end of my burgeoning social life, how would I keep up with Arsenal? There was no Internet, no blogs, no wall-to-wall coverage. And I could forget about actually going to games!

So, both unfortunately and somewhat inevitably, supporting Arsenal turned into a long distance relationship – and anyone who's ever been in one of those will tell you how they can work out, particularly for teenagers. What's more, by this time, I'd gone full teenager, and although Sky and the Premier League had turned up and were doing their best to turn football into what they thought was a cool product, I was drifting away from the game to find my own definition of cool by doing incredibly cool things like smoking cigarettes, drinking cider, and hanging around. I followed results less keenly, and given that most of my friends at school who actually had an interest in football were Aberdeen fans, I began to lose interest. I still vaguely kept up with results, but it was only for the biggest of games that I showed any real interest, and even then, it was very much a personal thing; I didn't know any other Arsenal fans in the wild north, so I generally confined my relationship to reading occasional match reports in the paper.

It wasn't until a few years later, in the summer of 1996, when I went to university, that I rekindled things, which as it turns out wasn't a bad time to rediscover an affinity with Arsenal. Being a football fan had changed. The Premier

League and Sky bonanza had turned football into a highly marketable and lucrative product; footballers were superstars, household names who were being fortunes. Fronted by those erstwhile bastions of respectability and taste, Andy Gray and Richard Keys, Sky had turned the football match into an event; one that, for me at least, took place in the pub. To their credit, they really did change football broadcasting, bringing a pizazz and excitement to their coverage.

As a freshman at university, I looked for ways to fit in and connect with people, so I started going to the pub to watch the football. I went to university in Scotland, but the Premier League juggernaut and the magical Sky dish meant that it didn't matter where in the country you were – you still got to watch your team. To begin with, I went on my own and nursed my way through a few pints in a quiet corner, watching whatever game happened to be on – it wasn't just Arsenal I wanted to see, I wanted to watch all of it. Then I started making friends with people, fans of other clubs. Ironically enough, one of the first people I started going to watch the football with at university was, yes, a Tottenham fan. This time, however, I wasn't looking to compete, and I'm still good friends with that person today (he actually asked me to go to the last North London derby at their place with him; I politely declined).

For us exiles marooned in Scotland by our studies, football had become a thoroughly social event. It was about going out, drinking beer, having a laugh, enjoying some banter with mates, but most importantly, seeing your team beat the other lot so you could mock them mercilessly. And considering this was the tail end of the 1990's, I was lucky enough to be able to do that a fair bit. It was all based around the big screen in the pub, which as an arts student with plenty of free time, suited me very well.

Then, in 1997, we started being shown this thing in the university library called Netscape Navigator. It was all rather confusing, and frequently didn't work very well, if at all, but it provided access to this other new thing called the World Wide Web ("a tool for learning", oh yes). It fascinated and puzzled me in equal measure, and I spent a lot of time playing with it, enthralled by the idea that I could swap data with people on the other side of the world. Of course, I never remotely saw the potential for what it would become, or I'd probably have retired by now, possibly even laden with Arsenal shares, but some people did see what it might be used for, particularly with regard to football. One of the earliest sites I remember visiting, Football365, still runs today and has turned into a media, betting, and advertising empire. And it's still a major source of football news.

After I graduated, I moved to Edinburgh and once again supporting Arsenal changed for me. This time it was more of an evolution. The reason I chose Edinburgh, and not Glasgow, or anywhere in England, was because we had friends there – but they were mostly friends I'd had at school; that's to say, not Arsenal friends. This time, however, there was to be no drifting away. I had Sky Sports at home now, with its glitzy, in your face coverage, that I'd watch for an hour before the game, and for at least as long afterwards for the analysis and post-match interviews. Then I'd fire up my dial-up modem, get on the web, and see what the match report on the BBC said about it and either glow in the praise lavished on my team after they'd done me the courtesy of winning, or wallow in misery had they shamed me. Actually reading all the opinions and finding out what was being said and by whom became a pursuit in itself; something in which I could happily immerse myself for hours on end.

And then, sometime in 2002, I discovered Arseblog, the website that changed the way I supported Arsenal permanently. Arseblog was well written, which I very much appreciated, but more importantly it was funny. It had rants, but they were good rants – the sort of rants I had – which was a new concept in the football writing that I'd spent any time reading. There were plenty of match reports on the web – plenty of earnest pieces about how wonderful or terrible the team had been, with serious analysis of the matches; but what was new, at least to me, was the humour; you came for the post-match report, but you stayed for the jokes.

Arseblog was also very engaging. It was an opinion piece about Arsenal that was written every single day; regardless of whether there had been a game the day before – I wanted to read it in the morning. Not really because I wanted to know what was happening in the world of Arsenal – I invariably knew that stuff from the plethora of other websites that were out there. But I wanted to get the funny, humorous take that Arseblog was so good at. It wasn't that it was irreverent, or quirky, it just appealed to my sense of humour, and obviously it helped enormously that I invariably agreed with the opinions expressed, which were generally very reasonable and not reactionary. They were passionately pro-Arsenal and its values, loyal to the club and its staff. These were qualities I liked to think I had myself.

The other thing about it was the comments; to start with, it was a relatively small community of people from around the world with whom I was able to instantly identify through the Arsenal connection: people from London, from Utah, from Canada, from Scotland, from Ireland, from Australia, from Wales. These people were Arsenal fans, but as well as that, they were also relatively tech-savvy early adopters of the web – another common interest. The comments weren't just about the football either; there was a mix of conversation covering a range of topics, and it was the first online community in which I really felt at home. It undoubtedly appealed to the university version of me that had been so taken with the entire concept. It didn't matter where I was, or that I didn't go to games very often, and since it was online, it wouldn't matter if I moved on again.

My own involvement with Arseblog came when I offered to help out with the technical side. As I recall, there was some problem with images not being displayed, and at the time I was a web developer, so offered my assistance. After that there were other little technical issues here and there that I helped out with, and then one day the comments system on the blog broke for the umpteenth time, so I wrote a new one – the Arseblog Arses. From there I was privileged enough to be asked to write the blog on occasions of holiday and such like. I can tell you now, given that it has to be written every day, it is extremely hard work. I've had the slightly more dubious pleasure of writing for Arseblog in the close season, when there's literally nothing to talk about, and yet it still happens – and people still demand it – day after day, year after year. It's really quite the achievement to have been doing it almost every single day, for ten years, and still be attracting new readers.

The other significant component to Arseblog was the forum, which quickly grew and became where I spent far more of my time than I care to think about (and certainly wouldn't admit to any of my former employers!). The forum was far from just football related – there were posts on all sorts of subjects, with friendly and knowledgeable people from around the world willing to give you an opinion or talk with you at any time of the day or night. It was very addictive, and very community spirited. An excellent example of this was when I wanted to spend my stag weekend in London for an Arsenal game. The weekend we'd chosen was Highbury versus Blackburn, which was hardly the most glamorous of games, but after a request made on the forum, I got nine tickets for me and my friends for that game, via Arseblog. Nine! These were people that had never met me in real life, and certainly hadn't met my friends. I remember meeting one of these extraordinarily generous people in the city to get his season ticket and not quite believing he was happy for me to post it back to him after the game. I tell you what, that was some responsibility – that ticket went back Royal Mail Special Delivery with extra insurance, and no mistake. That story really sums up the Arseblog community for me. Ten years later and I'm proud to say I'm still very much involved.

That hasn't been the end though. Twitter and Facebook have come along, both of which have given more fans more direct access to players than ever before. Twitter in particular was something I didn't see the point of until relatively recently, but I do appreciate the access it gives fans to players, at least theoretically, and to their credit, most footballers have embraced it too, sometimes with unintentionally hilarious consequences. But it's the web that changed everything when it comes to being a football fan. There are countless blogs, news sources, feeds, forums, chat rooms, and websites dedicated to clubs and players. It really makes no difference where in the world you live – you can be a supporter of whichever team you like. You can be an exile, an expat, and still watch your team. There are kids in China and Africa who have never seen Arsenal play live, and may never do so, that are some of the most passionate supporters out there; and I'm quite sure that like me, some of them are choosing to be Arsenal fans because their friends are Man United or Chelsea fans.

The clubs and players themselves haven't been slow to exploit the commercial potential this has brought – there's no doubt the web has contributed massively to the growth of the 'superclub', and players themselves are now global superstars. One or two players have even transcended their sport, David Beckham being the prime example, and while part of this is no doubt down to the general expansion of global media and the ambitions of companies like Sky and the Premier League, I think most of it is directly attributable to the web since it's made the world that much smaller and more accessible.

And as Arsenal fans I think we've been very lucky indeed that the age of the web-based fan has come along at a time in our history when we've been relatively successful and are playing attractive football. There's no doubt it has benefited the club enormously.

Here's to continued evolution.

Tom Clark is an Arsenal fan exiled in Edinburgh, Scotland. Occasional contributor to Arseblog, and creator of the arses, he looks after the technical side of the site.

7

HERBERT CHAPMAN

PHILIPPE AUCLAIR

Herbert Chapman; eternally plump, eternally anxious, no doubt, to undo a button of his well-filled and perfectly tailored waistcoat; eternally waiting to raise his homburg to a passing lady, does not correspond to the image we have of a football god. Luis-Cesar Menotti is a stronger candidate, long-haired like a doomed dueller, blessed with the kind of beauty men don't understand until it is too late to join the tango, something you would never have said of the Yorkshire man. Both smoked, but Herbert's cigarettes look stubbier than Cesar's on photographs somehow. Herbert didn't do sexy. But Herbert was a genius, not just the greatest manager Arsenal Football Club has ever had (which seems indisputable to me) but perhaps the greatest of them all; if greatness is ascertained not just in terms of a long intimacy with success, but also of a never-satisfied desire to move forward, innovate and experiment, whilst laying the foundations of traditions which long outlasted one's tenure at the helm of a club, or clubs, or national team.

Every Arsenal fan knows, or should know, that had it not been for Henry Norris turning to the man who'd just won two consecutive league titles with Huddersfield Town, their club might have gone back to the old second division from which they'd been very lucky (Tottenham fans might use a different adjective) to leave a decade earlier. None of the glories they witnessed in the 1930's, when the Arsenal had a legitimate claim to be recognised as the world's greatest team; in the early 1950's, when Tom Whittaker revived a club that had suffered more then most during WWII; in the late 1960s with McLintock's commando, or any time since, might be savoured now. Before Chapman made heroes of the Gunners, he saved them.

Look at the photographs again. Herbert has the appearance and the demeanour of a typical Englishman of his era; that of a prosperous merchant, perhaps, whose plate was only empty when he'd dealt with it with a robust fork. But within that wide, jovial and unremarkable frame, a brilliant, inventive, unorthodox, revolutionary mind was at work. I often wonder if there has ever been an English manager like him, and I sometimes despair that there will ever be another one (I very much doubt it). Chapman was a cosmopolitan, to start with. What would we not give to hear the conversations that he had with his great friends, the Austrian Hugo Meisl and the Italian Vittorio Pozzo? Imagine this, as I have, often: the man who offered W-M to England, then the world, the godfather of the Wunderteam and the architect of the Metodo, huddled around coffee cups and shots of brandy, somewhere in Vienna, Budapest, Trieste or London. These men were giants, their age a golden one, when modern football still had to be invented, which they did; for they were modernists, not plain modernisers.

Although an Englishman, Chapman was no little-Englander. Black players? Foreign players? So bloody what? When he was in charge of Northampton Town before WWI, he signed Walter Tull, the grandson of a Barbadian slave. The same Tull who'd played a handful of games for Spurs before he was hounded out of their first team by racist fans. (Somewhere in North London, there should be a statue of handsome Walter, the first coloured officer in the history of the British Army, who was killed in action in March 1918, three-and-a-half years after he volunteered to join the King's infantry; but that is a different story, one which should be taught in schools, and isn't).

Johnny Foreigners? He attempted to bring the great Austrian 'keeper Rodolphe Hiden to Highbury in 1930, only to have an unholy alliance of the Ministry of Labour, the PFA and the Football League squeal in unison and prevent the transfer from happening. Chapman then recommended Hiden to the only British manager who, in my opinion, deserves to be quoted in the same breath as Herbert, Jimmy Hogan. Hogan, who more or less brought modern football to the continent, coaching in the Netherlands, Austria, Hungary, Switzerland, Germany and France (only to be branded a 'traitor' by the FA) took Hiden to Racing in Paris, where he won one league title and three French Cups before Hitler's Wehrmacht passed the Maginot line. Chapman responded by taking on a Dutch 'keeper instead, the amateur Gerrit Keizer, who'd played a bit at one of Arsenal's feeder clubs, Margate FC, and regularly featured in Arsenal's first team in the 1930-31 season before his daring and idiosyncratic (euphemisms for 'crazy' and 'erratic') style cost him his place in the starting eleven

Chapman never shared the belief most of his contemporaries had in the innate superiority of the English game, and envied those continental colleagues of his who could take their teams into the Mitropa Cup. This competition, championed by Hugo Meisl, played a vital role in the spectacular progression of clubs like Austria Wien, Ferencvaros, and Sparta Prague in the late 1920s and the 1930s. Had he not brought his Northampton side to Nürnberg as early as 1909? Hadn't he mooted the idea of a genuine European Cup more than two decades before L'Équipe launched it in 1955? The Arsenal were considered to be the world's premier side, however, despite being denied a chance to prove it. The Gunners had to be content with regular trips

to Paris to play against French football's aristocrats, Racing;
trips which were instigated by Chapman of course, and
became one of the great sporting occasions in my country
in the pre-war years. Wishing to spare his players a strenu-
ous train and ferry journey, Herbert thought nothing of
flying to the French capital at considerable expense – the
first team to do so, one of so many 'firsts' linked to his
name – to ensure that James, Hulme, Bastin et al were in
peak condition to confront their opponents. It made perfect sense; but then, so many of Chapman's innovations,
all of them in fact, were based on common sense. What
set him apart was that he could distinguish prejudice,
which should be fought, from tradition, which must be
honoured, and that which was deemed 'revolutionary' by
others was only logical (he'd have used the word 'scientific')
to him.

Take his adoption of the WM system, which would
become the default tactical formation throughout most of
the world until Brazil introduced their 4-2-4 at the 1958
World Cup. The change of the offside law in 1925 led to
a glut of goals in the English League, and Arsenal's conventional 2-3-5 struggled to adapt to the new regulations.
Part of Chapman's genius was his astonishing attention to
detail, which led him to innovations like the adoption of
white sleeves and hooped socks, so that his players could
identify team-mates from close or from afar without losing
sight of the ball; but this arch-modernist was no control

freak. In fact, he'd go as far as encouraging his players to put forward tactical ideas at the weekly team meetings he'd introduced at Highbury; another first, it goes without saying. According to Brian Glanville, it was at one of these meetings that the great Charlie Buchan, a £2,000 snip buy from Sunderland, suggested that one of the three half-backs should drop between the two fullbacks to create a line of three defenders. The idea was not entirely new, and some recent research by Jonathan Wilson suggests that Southampton had played at least once in this formation in the 1923-24 season. But what might have been an experiment for others became a system for the Gunners once Chapman put Buchan's idea into practice, providing the organisational foundation on which Arsenal's ensuing success was built.

The way English football reacted to this tactical shift was two-fold – or, rather, borderline schizophrenic. Within a couple of years, almost every single professional club in the country had adopted Chapman's WM; but that didn't prevent opposing fans and supposedly neutral newspapers from accusing Herbert's serial FA Cup and League winners of practising an over-defensive football – and this, when Arsenal scored 127 goals to become champions in 1930-31. There is an explanation for this reluctance to give the Gunners their due: the watching public hadn't learnt to 'watch' yet. They still felt nostalgia for the short, triangular passing game favoured by legendary teams of the past such as

Corinthians, which the systematic use of the offside trap and the alteration of the laws had rendered obsolete a long time ago. By contrast, Arsenal, who had perfected the art of swift transition from defence to attack better than any other side of their era, favoured the 'long, well-placed kick' (Chapman's words – note: not the 'long ball') and the quick switching of flanks, in order to bring their opponents out of position with deadly effect. Chapman's players were also notably quicker, fitter and stronger than their rivals, thanks to their manager's unprecedented attention to diet and physical conditioning. Unfortunately, very little footage has survived of the conquering side of the 1930s, but what remains shows a team which, in terms of style, organisation and rhythm, is much closer to the implacable Liverpool of the early 1980's than to Pep Guardiola's Barcelona or, indeed, Arsène Wenger's Arsenal. This is not to say that Chapman discouraged his players from 'expressing' themselves on the pitch. The Scottish inside-forward Alex James, for example, had full licence to exploit his stupendous ability to pick passes that no other player could have imagined, yet alone executed – a Dennis Bergkamp in baggy shorts, if you will, with Cliff Bastin in the role of Freddie Ljungberg. Chapman was ahead of his time and, because of this, dominated it.

How far ahead he was can hardly be conceived in 2011, when it seems that there isn't much to be invented in football any more. We all know about the clock installed on the South stand, so that players and fans had a clear idea of how much time was left, something that, unbelievably, nobody had thought of before. This, by the way, is the reason why the giant screens at the Emirates show a 90-minute countdown, as intended by Herbert (and vetoed by the FA, as it would undermine the referee's authority, in their view), not the conventional clock you see in other grounds. Floodlights? Installed on the West Stand in 1932, vetoed by the FA, again, and only used for evening training sessions until 1951. Numbered shirts, white footballs, goal-line referees – all Chapman's ideas. Then there's the renaming of Gillespie Road tube station as 'Arsenal', a promotional masterstroke; his superb columns in the Sunday Express, designed to advertise the club as much as to enlighten their readers, and which are now, thankfully, in print again. No other manager had done such a thing previously. But then again, there'd never been such a thing as a 'manager' like Chapman before, a man who combined roles previously held by the club secretary, the head coach, the chief scout and, in many instances, the chairman himself. No aspect of Arsenal's life was too grand (the construction of the magnificent West Stand) or too inconsequential for him, down to the design of the new turnstiles (the first which provided a reliable head-count of the supporters who went through them) and scoreboard. He even thought of a new ticketing system, based on the one used on the London Underground, to cut queuing times. Ideas? "I would borrow one from a programme boy at Highbury, if it were a good one," he wrote.

Yet the greatness of Chapman doesn't stop at creating a near-invincible team and transforming a club, transforming football, in fact, through a considered, purposeful, and no less revolutionary for that, quest for innovation. It has been said of the former England cricket captain Mike Brearley that he had 'a degree in people'; in Chapman's case, that degree would have been a PhD. The outpouring of grief that followed his tragically early death on 6 January 1934 showed that he'd been loved as very few men who've wielded such power have been. His players loved the man as much as they respected the coach. He could be a strict disciplinarian, on one occasion deciding against signing a very talented footballer because of a dissolute lifestyle that ran against the values of Arsenal. But, far more often, he retained a 'human touch' that earned him the affection of his charges. He valued their input, as we've seen in the case of Charlie Buchan's championing of a new tactical system. He made sure they were well looked after, financially and otherwise; only the best hotels and the best restaurants would do; regular golf-outings were organised to provide relaxation and gentle exercise; but also to make these young men bond in a way that was quite out of the ordinary at a time when most professional footballers were treated as mere chattels by their clubs.

Chapman's elegance of manners also expressed itself in the way opponents were received at Highbury: he made sure that the floral displays which greeted visiting directors echoed the colours of their clubs, a tradition which has happily survived to this day, unlike, alas, the salute addressed to all four corners of the ground by the home team. Herbert wouldn't have liked the sign placed at the entrance of the London Colney training ground very much either, which reminds fans that they can't request autographs and that, in any case, the players have been instructed not to give any; a far cry from the days when young boys could turn up at Highbury and be invited to shake Alex James's hand in the dressing-room by Chapman himself.

Herbert the humanist – in the proper sense of the word, of a man who loved mankind – was also a supreme psychologist adept at using his gifts for the good of his club. You might have heard the story of how, on a trip to tempt away a player from a rival, he bribed a hotel barman to ensure that the drinks served to his companion and himself contained no alcohol whatsoever (despite ordering whisky and ginger ale, I believe) while those offered to his hosts would contain double shots of liquor. You may be less familiar with another Chapman tale; of how George Male was brought to his manager's office, fearing he'd be told that his services were no longer required, only to learn that he, a left-half, would be playing at right-back from then on. Male, who'd never played in that position – and remember this was an age in which tactical roles were far more rigidly defined than in ours – left Chapman's office convinced that not only would he be able to drop back one line and switch flanks, but that he'd become the best right-back in the country as well. Which he did, playing nineteen games for England in that position, six of them as captain, until the outbreak of WWII.

I've been fortunate enough to pass by Chapman's famous bust by Epstein at Highbury on many occasions, in the days before paranoia struck, when journalists were still allowed through the Marble Halls on match-days. I've never walked by without feeling a surge of pride for, and in, my club. He was ours: he transformed the Arsenal; he made champions of us. He made us. I also mourned him, and still do. If only in imagination, I'm one of the thousands who walked behind the hearse taking him to his final resting place in Hendon. What a blessing: the greatest creation of the greatest football manager of all, was and remains the Arsenal we love; and what sorrow, to know we shall never see his like again.

Philippe Auclair, France Football's England correspondent, regular contributor to The Blizzard and Champions, and author of Cantona - The Rebel Who Would Be King, has been a Gooner ever since he saw Liam Brady score that goal against Spurs. He also has a parallel career in music, under the name 'Louis Philippe'.

8

WHAT IS ARSENAL?

JULIAN HARRIS

What is Arsenal?

I put this question to a mass of Gooners on the popular Interweb forum, Twitter, and quickly gained a stream of pithy explanations of what fans associate with the club.

Some notable points from the findings:

Around one in six responses included the word, "class"

The same number mentioned, "tradition" and / or "heritage"

Even more mentioned Highbury, many specifying the Marble Halls

Several described, "doing things the right way"

A few included, "innovation"

Astonishingly, the most flattering and complete response came from a Leeds United fan, "You [Arsenal] have had the perfect balance between heritage, tradition and modernity," stated the gentleman simply known as Al.

Thanks, Al.

Admittedly, it was not the first compliment about Arsenal I've heard from a Leeds fan. A couple of hours after our boys trounced them 4-1 at Elland Road in 2002, a thick Yorkshire accent echoed across a town-centre pub's toilets, where I was busy removing several pints of ale from my system (they actually talk at urinals, up north, I have learned).

"You hammered us t'day," the friendly Leeds fan said.

'What a nice chap', I thought, and made some attempt at an affable, albeit awkward, response. "Yeah thanks, we, errr, we did ok."

But it wasn't over yet. The conversation, I mean. "The only thing I don't like about this Arsenal side," he continued – and then detailed a complaint so racist that my precious southern liberal conscience renders it unprintable. Suffice to say, our team that day included Kanu, Toure, Lauren, Campbell, Vieira, Wiltord, Cole and Henry. I'm sure you can work it out.

Bigotry aside, however, it was a cracking trip, and several thousand Gooners happily boarded trains back to the capital, all singing and lager-filled and what-have-you. But for every near-perfect away day like this, there is a dull and lengthy round-trip to witness a demoralising defeat, or some other annoyance. On driving back down the seemingly-never-ending M1-A1 after Sunderland's last-second equaliser in September 2010, I could not help but ask myself, 'What am I doing?'

Why had I just spent over £100 on yet another away game, to a stadium I'd already visited twice? Why was I so miserable? Why was I shouting expletives at Stan Collymore on the car's radio? Why didn't the defence just bloody hoof the ball clear?

But why did I care? Why do I have a red cannon tattooed for life on the left side of my chest?

Why did you buy this book?!

It is quite possible, Reader, that you too have pondered – or are pondering – such questions. For most of us, supporting the team is a continuation from childhood. To borrow from Fever Pitch: Arsenal winning trophies is the only thing we have consistently and passionately wanted since we were at school. Yet for children, it makes more sense. Children cling onto interests, suddenly and capriciously; they idolise certain adults; they dream about victory; they run around kicking a ball at any opportunity; they like wearing colourful outfits.

None of these things apply once we have become cynical, miserable, lazy and inactive adults. So why do we still bother? One answer was contained amidst my aforementioned Twitter survey. Too many people to ignore said either, "my dad" or, "my granddad" when asked what they most associated with Arsenal. I suspect in years to come that "mum" and "grandma" may enter the equation, but for now it seems that father/son footballing relationships remain dominant.

The rise of Internet genealogy in recent years is a symptom of people's on-going quest for continuity and heritage. Thankfully Arsenal provides us with tradition and heritage aplenty. Dare I suggest that our club is perhaps more wedded to its past than any other in England? Other clubs often point to one or two defining periods in their past; yet while the 1930's are assumed to be Arsenal's glory era, the team also won league titles in the 1940's, 1950's, 1970's, 1980's, 1990's and 2000's.

Moreover, the club's transition from one era to the next – from Chapman to Allison, from Graham to Wenger – is a mirror of the lineage of so many Arsenal-supporting families. The journey from one generation to another is often fraught with troubles, fall-outs and failings, yet the name stays intact and the DNA continues its evolution. Players, and some managers, quickly come and go; the club remains constant.

Yet this merely raises the need to examine our original question – What is the club? What is Arsenal?

Around two thousand years ago – even before Spurs last won the league – a Greek historian, philosopher and all-round intellectual type named Plutarch posed this conundrum: If a ship is repaired over a period of time, having each of its bits of timber replaced one by one, is it still the same ship?

The ship may look similar, and perform the same function, but all the timbers are different. In terms of its logistical, material make-up, Arsenal Football Club is at least 99 per cent different to when it was founded in 1886. The stadium is different, the training ground is different and players are different. Indeed, every fan is different. All the pieces have been replaced, several times over, during the club's long and varied history. Yet it is still the same club, right?

"We" moved to Highbury in 1913, didn't we? "We" won five league titles in the 1930's, right? That was Arsenal, the same club we still support, and not some alien historical entity. Fortunately for this chapter, I am firmly on the side of the ancient sophists who confident stood up and declared, "Yes, it is the same ship!"

The individual components of A Thing, I would argue, do not themselves comprise the meaning of The Thing. Rather, the meaning comes from how those components interact. And thus, even by changing those components entirely over time, if the replacement components combine to produce some kind of on-going effect, then The Thing is still the same Thing.

To put it another way, I'll paraphrase a more modern and less highbrow writer than Plutarch – Bill Bryson. Over the years of your life, the particles that make up your body replace themselves over and over again. You are losing particles right now. Yet you are still you. Whereas, if you sat there and unpicked each atom one by one from your body, with a pair of tweezers, you would just end up with an atomic cloud by the side of this book, that bore no resemblance to you whatsoever. It is not what you are made of that counts, it is how it all comes together.

In conclusion – Arsenal does still exist. Hurrah!

It is therefore little surprise that fans associate both themselves and the club with its history, and cling onto bygone eras. It gives purpose and backbone to the current, fleeting moments. You're not just watching a millionaire in a Nike top; you're watching a player who, whether he knows it or not, is continuing the unique innovation of putting white sleeves on red shirts. You're supporting the team with the cannon that harks directly back to the club's foetal period amongst the grimy machinery of the Woolwich Arsenal.

Arsenal, I feel, strive for identity and meaning more than other clubs, perhaps because we are not inherently and directly associated with a geographical location. On top of the departure from Woolwich almost a century ago, the club's modern-era names – both "The Arsenal" and "Arsenal" – suggest an entity several degrees above mere geographical concerns. Can you imagine a chapter of a book beginning: "What is Colchester United?" The second line would presumably read: "A football team from Colchester." End of chapter. The same goes for Newcastle United, Gillingham, Aberdeen, Olympique Marseille, et cetera.

I do not mean to belittle these clubs, each of which I am sure has a fascinating history, but there is undoubtedly something different about the Arsenal, reflected in its unique name. While the club is certainly now anchored in its Islington surrounds, and proudly established as north London's premier team, its legacy and meaning extends beyond this geographical pin – which is perhaps what attracts so many fans from throughout the world.

The respect for the club's history is on-going, with a new group of fans digging into the club's past and, even today, unearthing new evidence. Arsenal historian Tony Attwood, for example, believes that Henry Norris – controversial chairman and part-owner in much of the 1910's and 1920's – has largely been misrepresented and wronged by history's authors. "There should really be a statue of him outside the stadium," Attwood told me. "He's basically the club's founding father, arguably even more so than Herbert Chapman."

I spoke to Attwood and his colleague, Andy Kelly, about the ownership of Arsenal – another issue that seems to separate us from the norm. Arsenal is currently the only truly big club or top team in England that has not succumbed to being owned outright by some playboy kleptocrat or dubious group of businessmen. Despite Stan Kroenke accruing around two thirds of the Arsenal, independent owners, most of whom are fans, still own thousands of shares (around five per cent of the club). Supporters have created the new Fanshare scheme to boost fan-ownership.

In summary – several thousand fans own Arsenal stock, and have legal powers to hold the board to account. For much of the last century, the club was largely owned by dynasties such as the Bracewell-Smiths and Hill-Woods (another Arsenal quirk). Yet the club has a history of encouraging plurality of ownership right back to its genesis.

"Between 1886 and 1893 the club was run as a mutual co-operative," Kelly explains. "The club was owned by its members on a one-member-one-vote basis, it was run by a committee with a chairman who was voted for by the members. Anyone could be a member by paying a subscription."

In 1893 it became a Limited Liability Company with three-quarters of the shares up for grabs to the public. More shares were later issued, particularly when the club ran into financial trouble. Henry Norris "made very serious efforts to sell shares to people in Woolwich," according to Attwood. Norris told local fans that if they invested in the club, it would stay rooted in its locality. But the take-up was not sufficient, attendances were poor, and the club moved north of the river. Another share issue was conducted to raise money for the construction of Highbury, Attwood says, with a large amount bought by local north Londoners – presumably keen to disassociate themselves with that lot up the road. However, a lot of shares were lost through the decades, hence a large number of "orphan" shares, and the majority of the club became owned by the aforementioned well-to-do families, who finally sold out to David Dein, Danny Fiszman, and later Kroenke and Uzbeki Alisher Usmanov.

Supporter-ownership, in my opinion, is important and healthy for the club. For most fans, the relationship with the club extends well beyond watching a bunch of modern players and hoping they win over 90 minutes. It is a more permanent and, we hope, meaningful interaction. We are part of the club, like those bits of timber, each playing a part – often throughout most of our lifetimes – to contribute to its journey. This is why we drive to Sunderland, or Derby, or get on an extremely dodgy-looking ex-Soviet plane to attend a European Cup away game in Ukraine. And this is why, when asked, 'What is Arsenal?' on Twitter, we immediately think of the history, the heritage and even the ethics that we feel the club holds – or should hold.

Note the consistency in the responses: rather than people attaching their own supposed ethics to the club, fans generally gave the same responses. Arsenal means innovation, it means class, and it means doing things the right way. It is for this reason that the tragically-lost David Rocastle – officially my first favourite Arsenal player, even before Anders Limpar – is so embedded in Arsenal folklore, and celebrated for his famous imperative: "Remember who you are, what you are, and who you represent."

Despite becoming cynical, miserable, lazy and inactive adults, we still need hope. We still seek identity and enjoy being part of something bigger. Arsenal, irrespective of the team's up and downs, gives us all of this. More than just a team that represents a town, it is a club that we are all part of, with a unique identity, a strong heritage, yet also an unfettered enthusiasm for innovation and change.

This is why I am Arsenal, and I suspect it is why you're Arsenal, too. This is Arsenal.

Forward.

Julian Harris is a journalist, Arsenal season ticket holder and co-founder of the fan blog Gingers for Limpar. He Tweets (too frequently) about Arsenal @gingers4limpar.

9

LET'S GET DIGITAL

JAMES MCNICHOLAS

As little as ten years ago, the match day experience at Arsenal was markedly different – and not just because you were walking the narrow streets around Highbury rather than patrolling the Emirates' vast concourse. Yes, burgers were cheaper and the club shop was smaller, but whilst fans can now consume ground beef products and merchandise at ludicrous expense to their hearts content, there is something else they devour with equal fervour. Something that doesn't cost anything at all: information.

Today, a fan at the Emirates doesn't have to wait to see the teams emerge from the tunnel to know the starting line-up. He probably got the starting XI off Twitter whilst he was still in the pub. Not only that, but he was most likely able to read a microblog from Jack Wilshere detailing the extent of his ankle injury, as well as a projected recovery schedule. A new-fangled shiny stadium has coincided with a new-fangled shiny information age, in which we're all up to date, up to the minute, and up to our eyes in football. And this seems truer of Arsenal supporters than most. In the wide world of the web, Arsenal fans appear to be the most verbose, spawning literally hundreds of blogs, forums and online magazines each season. Take a look at the very book you're holding: so many of its chapters are con-tributed by those who began by self-publishing on blogs or other social media. The Editor? Arseblog, whose legs bestride the Arsenal blogosphere like a colossus.

For many of these writers, getting in to print was once a distant ambition, and their blogs a hopeful conduit to that goal. However, in the intervening years, digital media has begun to outstrip its physical counterpart. This is typified in the shift experienced by Arsenal's most renowned fan-zine: I suspect *The Gooner*'s online element receives many more hits than actual hard copies are sold. Football moves fast, and digital media allows writers to be responsive and reactive. A blog has the benefit of being editable right up to the whistle – and, crucially, it's free.

At the time of writing, the Wikio Blog Ranking (com-piled using traffic statistics and inbound links) lists seven Arsenal-specific sites amid their top 20 Football Blogs. Manchester United hold just one spot; the rest are made up of general interest football blogs, which of course are open to a far wider audience. Arsenal fans' voracious appetite for information seems to know no bounds. In the summer of 2011, for example, the previously unknown name of Costa Rican forward Joel Campbell trended globally as fans turned over every digital leaf for clues about his future. A 19-year-old footballer from Costa Rica became his country's most Googled citizen all on the back of some reported interest from Arsenal. What was once a curiosity has become a phenomenon.

Many have sought to understand just why Arsenal are so richly represented online – particularly those in the parasitic worlds of marketing and PR. I have dabbled in these areas myself, and have worked with some fantastic people, but any industry that uses the term 'viral' when talking about generating spread is bound to carry less than sanitary overtones and have, occasionally, less than sanitary practises.

One socio-economic theory is that Arsenal's inherent catchment area of North-East London contains an unusually high proportion of digitally literate 'new media' types. It's a suggestion that sits neatly alongside the modern perception of Arsenal as a middle-class club. It does not, however, reflect the true breadth or our fanbase, nor explain the wide variety of content produced by those who rarely set foot in this part of the world. Our man Arseblogger, for example, began his site whilst ensconced in the sunny sanctuary of Barcelona, and now lives in Dublin.

An alternative theory is that there is just something about our football club that provokes fans to put their thoughts down on paper, or some modern LCD-lit equivalent. I think we'd all like to believe that there is some element within Arsenal that fires a creative spark in its fans; that the crest is a muse, inspiring artistry in its followers as it does in its players. With some of the beautiful football we've been treated to in the past decade, that's almost credible – until you remember that most of the fans in question were raised on a steady diet of George Graham's football, when 'artistic' and 'inspiring' were less prominent epithets. I think the truth of it is far simpler: Arsenal had pioneers; brave explorers venturing in to the undiscovered country of the net. Arseweb was among the first, bringing fans news, results, and what today look like rather funky retro graphics. Though now inactive, it still stands as a totemic reminder of the Arsenal online creation myth.

And then came the blogs. The proliferation of information has meant that news, as a currency, has weakened. Original sources of stories are lost behind a carousel of re-tweets, as a literalised version of Chinese whispers plays out across the online playground. In this environment, where news is devalued, opinion is king. Into this void stepped Arseblogger, our foul-mouthed Christopher Columbus, accidentally unlocking a land of plenty. His sterling efforts and remarkable consistency made maintaining a weblog look easy. Inevitably, he inspired copycats. I can safely say that without Arseblog there would be no Gunnerblog. Without Gunnerblog there would be no ... well, perhaps that's a bad example, but you catch my drift. Like Johan Djourou's bizarre hairstyle, it's a pyramid that keeps on growing.

Arseblog, and the few sites that sprung up around it, established a culture of Arsenal blogging. Soon the sites were covering every aspect of the football club. Sociology dictates that any culture broad enough will eventually encompass subversion, and subcultures will be formed. With supporters hungry for more and more depth of knowledge, writers were able to carve themselves their own unique niches. Arsenal were the first club to sprout blogs about the youth and reserve teams, or to have their own unlicensed video highlights sites. The Internet has infamously allowed pornography to cater to specificity. Arsenal fans have embraced it similarly, fetishising the careers of players that ten years ago we simply would never have heard of.

For the club, the initial emergence of this chorus of online voices was something of a threat. Until then, the official website had been the sole authority on all things Arsenal: no dissenters, no discrepancy. Now they found themselves having to contend with a bunch of noisy, opinionated and increasingly influential independents. Relations between blogs and the press office were on the chillier side of lukewarm. To be fair to the club, their reaction was more of bemusement than belligerence. New media was exactly that – brand, spanking new, and no guidelines or etiquette existed explaining how to deal with them. With time, the frost has thawed and positive relationships have blossomed. The club have, if not embraced, then certainly offered a firm gentlemanly handshake to the unofficial sites, inviting them to be interviewed on Arsenal. com and initiating what ought to be a mutually beneficial affiliate scheme. Arsenal have gained a powerful ally and invested in a fertile new avenue in which to plant their press releases.

Moreover, it seems the club recognised that they too had to become a part of this digital world. On top of a redeveloped and more in-depth site, and initiating engagement with the blogs, they moved to create an official Arsenal Facebook page and Twitter feed. Of course, the sheer scale of the following of the official Arsenal channels means it's impossible for them to behave in a truly social way: they can't reply to every tweet, or 'Like' every Facebook comment. Instead, the club seem to have found an appropriate role as a concise authority: they are the definitive destination for news on the club. The blogs happily continue to buzz around them, satellites of speculation and conjecture, providing a voice for the fanbase.

The world of old media has followed suit. Newspapers now firmly encourage their journalists to join Twitter, interacting with fans to build and engage their audience. It's no longer good enough for Paddy Barclay of The Times to simply file a match report: he is obliged to tweet minute-by-minute observations, dissect the game during a live web-chat, and debate the controversial issues on *The Game* podcast. Engaging in this world has a benefit for journalists that goes beyond their employers' commercial interests; occasionally the better blogs can become sources for printed stories, in an inversion of the traditional media hierarchy. The landscape has changed. It's true that fans are still fans. Their opinion remains governed by one princeple factor; performances on the pitch. Changing the way they communicate has changed the football supporting experience irrevocably.

Take, for example, the instantaneous speed at which opinions are now transmitted. Views that would once have been lost amidst the roar of the terraces can now be digitally amplified. When the originator of those views has a significant following, it intensifies the effect. Inevitably, consensus forms faster, and a musing or rumour can quickly become an accepted wisdom. Footballers are overhyped, or written off, more swiftly than ever before. What was once a steady drip-drip of exposure is replaced by the equivalent of standing before a fire-hose.

This has had a direct impact upon the team and the atmosphere within the stadium, and more than one player has been caught in the blast. A memorable example is the now infamous booing of Emmanuel Eboue against Wigan in December 2008. In the months prior to the game, an online discourse had accelerated surrounding the player's perceived poor attitude and application. Now, I'm not naive enough to believe that every supporter in the Emirates on that day was part of the online community around the club, nor am I discounting the ability of fans to judge what they see with their own eyes. However, the unprecedented degree of impatience and rage directed at a player in our own colours was undoubtedly characteristic of the online debate. The ill-feeling towards the Ivorian had built up on the Internet and spilled in to the Emirates. In the interest of balance it's important to point out that it was an initially ironic online movement that subsequently turned Eboue in to a joyful Internet meme, beginning the slow process of restoring his reputation at Arsenal. Until he ruined it again.

I don't mean this theory of the potential for nigh-instantaneous consensus should lead you to believe Arsenal fans are all one happy family, sitting around a figurative camp-fire holding hands and singing "Kumbaya" to the strum of imaginary ukuleles. The hive-mind is not without its divisions. A glance at the work of Arsenal's voluntary chroniclers will show you a diverse range of opinions on the direction of the club, the board, and above all the manager. There are plenty of fascinating and genuinely worthwhile debates, and here we encounter another strength of the medium – the opportunity for interaction and response. For the most part, opposing views are expressed eloquently and respectfully. Unfortunately, that's not always the case.

The bigger your stadium is the more pigeons will gather in the rafters to shit on you from the darkness, and as Arsenal's online universe has grown, so has it begun to include some rather unsavoury elements. Conflict, history will tell you, is a necessary counterpart to expansion.

Take Twitter, which works as a microcosmic example of this trend. As an up-and-coming social network, it was once the preserve of erudite media folk – the landed gentry of the online world – who crafted their 140 character messages with elegance and wit, gaily skipping through the digital meadows and high-fiving each other as they swapped #FFs back and forth. In recent months, however, it seems someone has opened a portal from the online asylum that is YouTube comments. Into Twitter have poured the trolls and other creatures that surely belong only in Norse mythology, spouting bile and throwing insults and tantrums in equal measure. It is a pattern reflected across the web. Eventually, these Internet hooligans will find you.

I don't, of course, mean you, dear reader. In purchasing this book alone you have demonstrated yourself to be a considered and excellent sort. I am certain you are reading this on some idyllic veranda, chugging peacefully on a pipe whilst planning a scheme to simultaneously end world hunger and the recession. There are, however, less discerning Arsenal fans out there; ones capable of mutating debate into division. Tribal behaviour is common in both football and online communities, so we ought not be surprised by it, but it's a shame when Arsenal fans turn on each other. A spectrum of opinion is reductively bludgeoned into a two-way scrap.

In the eyes of some, fans fall into one of two categories: either in thrall to the Gallic charms of Arsene Wenger, or one whose outlook is that of permanent doom. Inevitably, it is the negative shouts that are heard loudest. It's a shame, because the animosity threatens to turn what ought to be an erudite assembly in to a mud fight. The tribalism in football fans is most productive when directed outwards, not inwards. It ought to be "Us vs Them", not "Us vs Us". It's also something of an abuse of the opportunity for collaboration and communication presented to us.

I opened up by talking about how the match-day experience has shifted for those inside the ground, but the most dramatic changes have been for those fans outside the borders of the stadium and, even more so; the country. Arsenal have millions of fans across the world, and only 60,000 of them can file through the Emirates' electronic turnstiles. There are plenty outside of these confines who are equally as committed, and just as heartfelt in their support. They kick every ball in Beirut, and feel every tackle in Tokyo. The incredible response of the fans in Asia during our tour in the summer of 2011 seemed a surprise to players and staff alike, but won't have been to webmasters who've witnessed a consistent flow of traffic to their sites from that part of the world. The game has gone global, and Arsenal have too.

The online activity I've described acts as both the fuel and the evidence of that growth, feeding an ever-expanding frenzy. Gooners all around the globe are closer to the game than they've ever been before, able to follow Arsenal without missing a beat. Local fans benefit too. The emergence of Twitter is reversing the economics-driven alienating effect that threatened to destroy the bond between players and fans. Now there are opportunities for genuine interaction with our heroes, which seemed unthinkable only a few years ago.

We're all joined up; players, fans, and journalists, and more. In the case of Arsenal, it is an incredible community, unmatched in English football, and I'm delighted to have spent almost a decade as part of it. Arsenal built the Emirates for 60,000; the web has built a stadium that can hold us all. But there are no stewards here: let's not let the infighting spoil it for ourselves.

James McNicholas began blogging about all things Arsenal at Gunnerblog.com in 2004.

10

ALL HAIL THE ALMOST INVINCIBLES

CHRIS HARRIS

What makes some title teams more memorable than others?

Drama, for starters. What Arsenal fan will ever forget Anfield '89, Mickey Thomas, 'It's up for grabs now!' and all that? Then there's the venue. Win the league at White Hart Lane or Old Trafford and you can brag about it forever. So that's 1971, 2002 and 2004 covered, in case you needed reminding. A long wait for glory also lubricates the celebrations. Arsenal supporters were positively gagging for the title after the 18-year hiatus in 1971 and, coincidentally, the same delay before 1989; while a seven-year itch was scratched in 1998.

Of course there's history too. Turn a title into a Double – as Arsenal did in '71, '98 and '02 – and there's less chance of it falling down the back of your memory bank. And if you go an entire season unbeaten … well, that pretty much guarantees immortality. So spare a thought for the class of 1991. It's more than 20 years since George Graham's squad cavorted around Highbury with the championship trophy – not to mention a rather uglier pot from the sponsors – but this particular title can slip the mind when Arsenal fans recall the highs of their supporting lives.

Why? Well, the '91 success wasn't laced with drama: Arsenal wrapped up the title with two games to spare. It wasn't won at the home of a fierce rival; in fact, Graham's side wasn't even on the pitch when they became impossible to catch. The fans, though ever grateful for a title to celebrate, were hardly strangers to the experience after the magic of Anfield two years prior (the chance to Double-up was scuppered by an uncharacteristic cup blip). Without the special ingredients needed to extend its shelf life, the '91 title can get overlooked when the conversation turns to Arsenal's finest. But that's unfair because the statistics and circumstances suggest that Graham's second championship team was as potent as any post-war Gunners' side – with the possible exception of the bar-raising, history-shredding Invincibles.

Ah, the Invincibles. We'll never forget them, will we? And yet they might have been scrabbling around for another label had a depleted Arsenal side nicked another goal at Chelsea in February 1991 and avoided the solitary league defeat they suffered that year. Yes, Graham was that close to beating Arsene Wenger to the punch by 13 years. Either way, his team did suffer fewer defeats than any other top-flight side in the 20th century – a magnificent achievement.

Assuming some readers weren't old enough – or even alive enough – to enjoy the 1990/91 campaign in all its majesty, it's worth recapping how Arsenal won the league. They had, frankly, flopped the previous season following that incredible high at Anfield in '89, but were re-energised by a clutch of new signings – David Seaman, Anders Limpar and Andy Linighan – not to mention the hunger of those who had missed out on the World Cup finals in Italy. Tony Adams, Alan Smith and David Rocastle all failed to make the cut when Bobby Robson named his England squad and the Arsenal captain felt he had a point to prove. "Being omitted from the squad that summer probably did me, and perhaps even Alan and David, a power of good in Arsenal terms. I was fresh and full of determination to prove people wrong," Adams wrote in his autobiography, Addicted.

Having formed a strong pre-season bond in Scandinavia, Arsenal hit the ground running in August. Wimbledon were beaten 3-0 at Plough Lane on the opening day (a good omen: Graham's side kicked off their 1988/89 campaign in the same manner at the same ground) and the Gunners eventually hauled in early pacesetters, Liverpool, inflicting the champions' first league defeat of the season in December. They did so in style as Paul Merson's cute back-heel set up Smith for a show-stealing strike to clinch a 3-0 win at Highbury.

Arsenal led the First Division by New Year's Day and eventually stretched their club record unbeaten run from the start of the campaign to 23 games, before going down at Chelsea in February. But they atoned for that aberration at Anfield a few weeks later as Seaman kept John Barnes and company at bay before Merson's cool finish earned a decisive 1-0 win. It represented a changing of the guard as Liverpool, for so long the dominant force in English football but unsettled by the resignation of manager Kenny Dalglish, ceded power to Graham's men. That was no mean feat: for anyone growing up in the Eighties, Liverpool had been pretty much untouchable at home and in Europe.

Arsenal looked set for a Double and, although those dreams were extinguished by Tottenham in a horrible FA Cup semi-final at Wembley, the title duly arrived on May 6 in rather more humdrum circumstances than one might have expected. Liverpool's defeat at Nottingham Forest meant that Graham's team were champions when they took to the pitch to face Manchester United an hour later at Highbury. Smith scored a hat trick in a 3-1 win to edge himself closer to the Golden Boot, but, next to the drama of Anfield '89, this had the air of an exhibition match. By the time the champagne corks had popped and the parade around Islington was in full flow, the bare facts were these: Played 38 Won 24 Drew 13 Lost 1 For 74 Against 18 Goal Difference +56 Points 83.

The stingiest defence in Arsenal history got the plaudits and rightly so – no other top-flight side has kept as many as 24 clean sheets nor conceded as few as 18 goals. The quartet of Lee Dixon, Tony Adams, Steve Bould and Nigel Winterburn had lined up together for the first time in 1988 and, after two years of Graham-flavoured intensity and repetition on the training pitch they were a fearsome unit, with a strong supporting cast in David O'Leary and Linighan.

Then there was Seaman. Arsenal fans had been up in arms about the proposed move for the Queen's Park Rangers goalkeeper in 1990 – "We all agree, Lukic is better than Seaman" was a regular refrain on the Highbury terraces – but Graham knew what he was doing. "I still think John Lukic is one of the top five keepers in the country. I just think David Seaman's the best," he insisted. And he was right, of course, proving his players wrong as well as some supporters. "I had not realised David was as good as he was when he was at QPR," wrote Adams in Addicted. "And the defence was so familiar, it was practically unbreachable at times. Steve Bould was simply outstanding. In footballing terms he was next to impassable." Winterburn agrees: "Nothing will have the drama of the 1989 title but 1991 was special because in particular the back four was built-in," he recalled. "At that time I felt it was impossible to go unbeaten but we gave it a good shot. Under George we were just a clinical team that had the right formation to win; we were almost a machine."

Arsenal's defensive meanness was legendary. But perhaps more surprisingly, the '91 vintage scored more times than the revered, free-flowing Invincibles and boasts the best goal difference of any post-war Arsenal side. Another of Graham's defensive kingpins, Bould, thinks that side's attacking verve is too often overlooked. "Rocky [Rocastle] was still at the club, Mickey Thomas was there, Paul Davis too, we had some talented footballers, it wasn't just about the defence and keeping clean sheets," he says. "The style was rather rigid because that's the way George wanted us to play – he wanted it tight, he wanted to win 1-0 and not 4-3. But as it happened we had good players and we scored a hell of a lot of goals that season – I think we scored a lot of fours and fives as well as a six against Coventry on the final day. It was a good side, we were tight at the back and we had some flair up front."

As it happens, Rocastle, so influential two years earlier, spent much of the 1990/91 campaign nursing injuries, but Thomas and Davis offered energy and vision from the centre, while Merson's pace and flair complemented the prolific Smith's more prosaic qualities up front. As is often the case, one or two players emerged during the season to play a notable role: for Nicolas Anelka, Chris Wreh and Alex Manninger in 1998, read David Hillier and Kevin Campbell in 1991. The former added ballast to the midfield while the latter's raw power and pace was a sight to behold when he broke into the Arsenal side during the run-in. It certainly might surprise those who saw Campbell labouring towards the end of his career.

And of course there was Limpar. Signed from Italian side Cremonese for £1million, the original 'Super Swede' was Graham's trump card and, in the words of commentator Martin Tyler, "the man they are calling their new match winner". Limpar sprinkled magic dust on Arsenal's title charge, scoring and making goals, while bewildering defences up and down the country. In a time when overseas signings still had a novelty value, before the trickle of imports became a flood, Limpar's flair and freshness turned heads. "We had Anders to give us that little bit of magic," recalls Bould. "The first time we actually saw him in a game was in the pre-season Makita Tournament at Wembley in 1990. He scored against Aston Villa, he smashed this one into the top corner having beaten about 18 players and we thought, 'Jesus Christ! Who's this kid?' Anders wouldn't have really been George's kind of player, or so we imagined, but he had that magic about him and it's quite sad that he didn't go on and have a seven or eight-year career at Arsenal. He looked like he was going to be a real top player year-in year-out for the club, he was like a little George Best when he first arrived and he was brilliant for 18 months to two years but then never really pushed on." Winterburn was a big fan too. "We met up with Anders in Sweden and he had great ability, really quick feet. He was absolutely sensational at the start of his Arsenal career; defenders could not get near him for long periods of games with his movement. He had pace as well and was a terrific player to play alongside. We were very organised, we pressed, we were hard to beat, and we were introducing a little bit of flair with Anders."

There's a tendency to lump the class of '91 in with Graham's cup kings of 1993 or even the side that conquered Europe a year later. But while those later sides leant heavily on defensive resilience and relied on Ian Wright to nick a goal, the '91 team had verve in abundance. This was a time when Graham still trusted the likes of Limpar and Rocastle and picked passers as well as destroyers in midfield. That tally of 74 goals in 38 league games speaks for itself.

So if the '91 side was dazzling as well as doughty, why else does it get overlooked? Bould thinks the timing of Arsenal's triumph and the perception of the club back then are partly responsible. "We were very good that year," he says. "We played every week thinking we couldn't lose, there was a confidence about everybody. But people didn't love football so much back then, the Premier League hadn't formed and the game had yet to explode. All the exposure now is above and beyond what it used to be and I'm sure that's one of the reasons why that '91 team didn't get that much notice. Football had been in troubled times, it was just coming out of the doldrums and all the attendances were nowhere near what they are now. On top of that we were everybody's hated team at that time. I think Liverpool were perceived as the club that could play football while we were perceived to be journeymen and cloggers and not too pretty."

Arsenal were certainly not as lovable then as they would be under Wenger and, although new football supporters had been wooed by Paul Gascoigne's tears and England's exhilarating run to the 1990 World Cup semi-finals, the toxic reputation the sport had built up during the Eighties would need slightly longer to shift. The razzmatazz of the Premier League – launched a year after Arsenal's title success – brought families as well as casual fans on board. But at the turn of the decade it was less acceptable to like the team they called 'Boring, boring Arsenal' – a mocking chant that was ironically adopted by Gooners once Wenger, Dennis Bergkamp and the rest, had deliciously made their mark.

After the excitement of Italia '90 – at least from an England perspective – perhaps the new wave of football fans weren't ready for a team as supposedly rugged and methodical as Graham's, or at least a team so dominant that drama was in far shorter supply than it had been in Turin when Bobby Robson's side took on West Germany. A penalty shoot-out, larger-than-life personalities, a famous old rivalry and a dash of jingoism can capture the imagination where a 38-match machine-like march to the title cannot. Let's be honest: for better or worse, Graham's Arsenal did not boast a personality or superstar like Gascoigne. The '91 title side was put together on a relative shoestring, with only the fees for new signings Limpar, Seaman and Linighan creeping into seven figures. And although Arsenal had the flair of Limpar, Merson and Rocastle, the foundations of their success – organisation, efficiency and collective strength – were reflected in the end-of-season awards. Gordon Strachan of Leeds and Manchester United duo Mark Hughes and Lee Sharpe walked off with the individual gongs while Arsenal's own success remained very much a team effort. If you want more evidence, pop in your 'Champions' video from the 1990/91 campaign (kids, ask your parents about this) and fast forward (ditto) to the 5-0 win over Aston Villa late in the season. After surging into a four-goal lead you might expect Arsenal to ease off slightly but their harrying and tackling is as committed as ever, even when the game is won. Teamwork, flair, a miserly defence and a potent strike-force – is that enough for the '91 team to be mentioned in the same breath as the finest Arsenal sides? If you're still not convinced then consider this: it's likely that no other title team has overcome such adversity in their quest for the championship.

Graham's squad endured two savage blows in 1990/91 that could easily have derailed their ambitions and may well have proved terminal for lesser sides. First of all, their inspirational captain spent eight weeks of the season in prison after being found guilty of drink-driving. Jailed on December 19, Adams missed eight games – that's more than 20 per cent of the league programme – before making his top-flight return at Anfield of all places. Would the 'Invincibles' have been invincible had Patrick Vieira spent 58 days in Chelmsford nick? Would history have been made in 1971 if Frank McLintock had been locked up for that long? Given that football is a game of fine margins, given that both were totemic figures, there would be plenty in the 'no' camp for that debate.

The 1991 side just got on with it. Linighan is best known for his 1993 FA Cup final heroics but he came in from the cold to partner Bould and help keep Arsenal's title challenge on track. "I have to say that the biggest praise you can ever give is to Andy Linighan," says Bould. "He had just been bought from Norwich for what was then considered a fair bit of money and he didn't get straight into the team and he found it tough. Then Tony went to jail and in came Andy and it looked like he'd been involved in the system we were so used to since he was a kid. In many ways Tony wasn't missed and that's high praise for Andy. As for myself, well, I have to say I enjoyed the extra responsibility. No team is ever a one-man team, I don't care who it is. Barcelona are not just Lionel Messi. Everybody has a job and sometimes you have to pitch in and if our captain was missing then you have to have a go." It's worth pointing out that Adams' incarceration coincided with Arsenal's sole defeat of the league season – that 2-1 reverse at Chelsea. Would that have been avoided, and history made, if the captain had been around? Quite possibly.

Adams wasn't the only one in trouble that season: the entire club found itself in the dock in the wake of the infamous Old Trafford brawl. It all kicked off during the first half of

Arsenal's 1-0 win in October – secured by an audacious strike from that man Limpar – with only Seaman keeping his distance while protagonists and peacemakers pushed and protested. The Football Association came down hard on both clubs but especially Arsenal, docking them two points. It was an unprecedented punishment and one at which Bould still bridles. "It was ridiculous," he says. "It certainly wasn't worth two points for misconduct, it was an absolute joke, it was a few handbags at dawn. It was ridiculous but again we weren't a very well-liked club at the time, I think people thought Arsenal were a bit stuffy but I don't know why. Two points off was scandalous." Winterburn admits that the residual bad feeling between the sides probably stemmed from his run-in with Brian McClair during an FA Cup tie at Highbury in 1988. "I was involved in the tackle with Denis Irwin that started it all off but what went on after that wasn't my fault," he says. "I was lying on the ground and I got a couple of kicks in the back and fair play because it was competitive. It did seem harsh to have points taken away but maybe the FA wanted to set a precedent. We just felt 'it's happened, let's get on with it'."

And get on with it they did. Arsenal's domination rendered the points deduction obsolete – they could have had another seven removed and still been crowned champions. Once again, one has to ask if other sides might have responded differently to such a sense of injustice. The Invincibles, for example, saw their title defence crumble after a handful of bad refereeing calls brought their record 49-game unbeaten run to an end at Old Trafford in October 2004. Would they have been shaken or stirred by a points deduction? We'll never know, of course, but this is certain: the '91 side had the character to turn a negative into a positive by using their punishment to foster a siege mentality within the squad. "George loved it to be fair," recalls Bould. "Every day when we came in he'd remind us that people didn't like us. 'It's us against the world,' he used to say. We had that kind of siege mentality as a group." Adams agrees. "What happened at Old Trafford spoke volumes about our character," he wrote in Addicted. The captain demonstrated Arsenal's 'us versus them' mentality in a less-than-subtle manner when he flicked V-signs at QPR's fans after a late comeback at Loftus Road a matter of days after the points deduction had been handed down. And the fans soon joined in. One of the most boister-ous chants at Highbury on the day Arsenal won the title? "Stick your two points up your arse!" Fittingly, Manchester United were the visitors.

Those incidents did nothing for Arsenal's reputation of course and that's one reason why the Invincibles will always win a popularity contest with the '91 vintage. But they have more in common than you might think. For start-ers neither side fulfilled its potential. Thirteen years before Wenger's team squandered a golden chance of Champions League glory by running out of steam against Chelsea,

Graham's men fluffed their lines in that FA Cup semi-final against a Gascoigne-powered Spurs. Having won their respective titles so convincingly, neither side could live up to their own high standards in the years that followed. "That was a big disappointment," admits Bould. "The following year was a really poor year. We never got going in the league until it was too late and, although we had the cup successes in 1993 and 1994, the group should have done better than it did."

All the same, the '91 team deserves to be held in the same high regard as that most revered of Arsenal sides. It was more secure in defence; more productive up front and so nearly cornered the market in invincibility long before Thierry Henry was cutting a swathe through defences. If Ruud van Nistelrooy had smashed his penalty six inches lower in September 2003, if Adams had been a free man in February 1991 … on such fine margins are legends built. Not that Bould is overly concerned. "It could have been us but I'm not sure I like the tag anyway!" he says. "Everybody gets carried away giving people and teams and clubs tags. We didn't have the style of the Invincibles team – they raised the bar I think – but although we weren't as exciting to watch as some of Arsene Wenger's teams, we had good players, we were a really good unit and perhaps we never got the praise we should have done."

So it's time to put the record straight and finally give the '91 side the credit it deserves. They weren't just another title side; they were special. The stats and conditions of their triumph bear that out. If you don't think great achievements are ever forgotten, remember this: when Arsenal fans were asked to pick their favourite centre backs of all time in an online poll in 2011, Frank McLintock – the inspirational Double-winning skipper of '71 no less – could not even force his way into the top five. Old-school legends get edged out by modern-day heroes, and if the high-water mark of Graham's reign is already hazy, those recollections will fade even further as the years roll on.

Anniversaries of Arsenal's most significant moments keep those memories alive. In 2011 the club quite rightly marked 40 years since its first Double and a decade since the tragic death of David Rocastle. But strangely, there was no celebration of the team that broke records and made history in 1991. So please don't forget Graham's finest. They might not have been the most attractive Arsenal side of all time – but they might just have been the most effective.

Chris Harris has worked for Arsenal since 2002. His Dad took him to his first game at Highbury in 1983 – it was Tony Adams' debut – and he can never thank him enough.

11

ARSENAL AND FAMILY

SIAN RANSCOMBE

I am from an Arsenal family. I mean, I suppose we are all from an Arsenal family collectively, but I have the double whammy, like many of us, of having also grown up in a house full of Arsenal supporters. There are both pros and cons to this situation. The pros are, of course, that there is no ribbing from any annoying little Spud brothers post-defeat, nor any dinnertime debates as to whether Ferguson is better than Wenger. Also, following a big win, it's like the button of loveliness has been pressed – everyone is happier, morning cereal tastes better, the house feels brighter, the sofa cushions feel fatter. The cons on the other hand, are that there is no escaping the misery when times are tough. None whatsoever.

My sister has actually been known to announce at the beginning of a family gathering: "There will be no football discussion tonight". It's not because she doesn't like football – she loves it – it's simply for the sake of our own sanity. Shepherd's pie turns into a board meeting. Sausage hotpot becomes an argument over who is being deluded and who is being a doomer-gloomer. It is a fundamental part of life in the Ranscombe house, and has been for a long old time.

In spite of having Arsenal in the veins, my sister and I were never pushed into becoming Gooners. It might seem a bit sexist but maybe if we'd been boys we'd have been straight up to Highbury as soon as our little legs could toddle. I knew I was an Arsenal fan and that they played in red and white and that I was supposed to cheer for them, but that was about as far as it went. I even remember seeing interviews with Le Boss back in 1996 (I was seven), and seeing the words 'Arsène Wenger, Arsenal Manager' underneath, and truly believing 'Arsène Wenger' was French for 'Arsenal Manager'. When I realised this was not the case – though in a way I still feel like it is – I simply assumed that Arsenal had been named after him. My first ever match at Highbury came in August 2000, against Charlton Athletic. We won 5-3. I went with my mum, my dad and my sister. I remember climbing the stairs to the West Stand and catching my first glimpse of the pitch. It was one of the most beautiful things I'd ever seen, and I mean that to sound a lot more genuine than I'm sure it does.

My mum Teresa, who is from Holloway Road, went to her first match on Boxing Day in 1966 with her Uncle

Patsy and her brother Kevin. She and Kev were sent in through the schoolboys' entrance with two shillings (10p, apparently). Once through, there was a gate to the North Bank manned by a steward. If the steward knew your dad or your uncle, he'd let you through. By comparison, for my first match we had the tickets in our hands days before kick off. No stewards recognised my dad and 10p would have got me no further than a tenth of a bag of sweets from the man who sells them outside the stadium.

Being local, Mum and her brother also used to hang around on a Friday afternoon and wait for autographs as the players arrived to training. In those days, unlike now with the underground car parks and the enormous newly built training facilities, the players would park their cars on Avenell Road. She was always really impressed by goalkeeper Jim Furnell's car, which was a Ford Capri Ghia. Nowadays, Jack Wilshere's shiny bright Mercedes-whatever-it-is is pretty much a standard first or second car for a footballer. One of Mum's favourite away day memories was going to White Hart Lane in 1971. They had never been before and arrived to learn that the match was sold out. So, naturally, they climbed over the fence to get in. As they clambered, they were almost caught by the hooves of a police horse. Contrast this to my first away match, at Craven Cottage in 2003, where I remember wondering if the Tube journey there would ever end. If there were police horses there that day, they certainly didn't do any wall climbing (nor did I, in fairness … my mother was a far braver young woman than I). Her childhood hero was Ian Ure, swiftly followed by Bobby Gould. My childhood hero, and probably the man that made me fall in love with the Arsenal first, was Patrick Vieira.

Being such a huge Arsenal supporter and coming from a family from which liking football is as much a requirement as having our surname, there is that extra ingredient I'll have to look for when thinking about the husband and children of the future. I don't want Chelsea supporting kids – how would I love them? Mum was fortunate enough to have found my dad Alan, who is probably the biggest Arsenal fan I know. When Cesc Fabregas left the club recently, it felt like a punch to the brain. We are huge Cesc fans and my good-bye-to-Cesc blog was the most difficult I've written, but I still think Dad summed up the feeling of the sad football fan the best with this comment: "I just get annoyed when people don't love my club as much as me." And isn't that exactly it? Players can come and go, but we can't. Or won't.

Anyway, my dad is also an Islington boy, having grown up on Gillespie Road itself. His dad – my Granddad Billy – passed away in December 2005. The fact that Highbury, their local stadium, had been plastered with the words 'The Final Salute' ahead of our move to the Emirates that season, seemed very apt indeed. Granddad Billy was a fan, because his dad was a fan. As were his brothers Henry and Fred. My Granny, on the other hand, is from Broughty Ferry in

Scotland. Her first match at Highbury came in 1935, a 6-0 win over Grimsby Town. She was on holiday in London with her mum. Coincidentally, Granddad was there at the match too, and was stood in the very same stand as she and her mum. They didn't eventually meet until 1941, up in Scotland. Very selfish of them that they didn't meet on that great day for the Arsenal in 1935, thus enabling their first-born granddaughter to tell the world 'My grandparents met at Highbury!' but you can't have it all.

We're of varying degrees of positivity in this family, with my dad and I probably being the most irritatingly upbeat about our predicament no matter the details. There's a part in Fever Pitch where Nick Hornby discusses always wanting reassurance from his dad that everything was going to be OK at a match. I know this feeling. I do exactly the same to mine. I can be quite sure of my views and predictions and feelings about a match, but even now at the age of 22, I always need reassurance from my dad that everything is going to be OK. That's another one for the pros list of being from an Arsenal family. I look at people who have chosen to support this club for reasons other than genetics and I can't get my head around it. Who do you go to for reassurance? How do you know it is going to be OK? How do you know you have permission to curse and twitch your way through a football match, knowing that everyone will understand that it's only the gut-shredding nerves making you behave so out of character?

As established in the opening lines of this little ramble, 'Arsenal and family' is not just about your actual nearest and dearest. Though there have been many occasions of out and out civil war among supporters in both recent and not-so-recent times, the feeling of being among fellow supporters is a bit special. The home crowd at the Emirates is often on the receiving end of a lot of criticism for not being vocal or passionate enough. This gives me the hump for two reasons: Firstly, because it's often quite true. There are, for instance, a group of men who sit near me at the stadium and whose voice boxes seem only reactive to the setting 'whinge'. There's no other word for it, they whinge. They are whingers. Whinging is what they are good at, and so they whinge. They don't sing, they don't shout out anything positive, they just sit there analysing the game like a teacher analysing a child's report card.

'SILLY, Jack! Oh for goodness' sake, this is winnable in the middle!'

Winnable in the middle? Who uses that many syllables at a football match? The other reason it's annoying is that there are plenty of people who do come away from each match with no voice left. When people make comments like 'Arsenal's support is rubbish', you just have to roll your eyes as hard as when someone suggests we still need a new goalkeeper. When you factor in the vast amount of support we have from overseas as well, I wonder if waking up at the crack of dawn on a Saturday morning because you happen to live half a world away from London, could be considered a sign of passion? Or if being physically unable to get to sleep after a particularly amazing late night of football has left you more bursting with adrenaline than a BASE jumper means you might care just a little bit? Back in London, even Whingey McGrumble behind me is dedicated enough to show up to every match. It might not contribute much to the atmosphere, but support is support.

I've been fortunate enough to have only really seen the good times of the Arsenal so far. They've given me beautiful memories, more than anyone should really be entitled to in the cruel world of competitive sport. Two doubles (that I can remember); The Invincibles; European nights of beauty; the Sol goal in the Champions League final; Barcelona at home last season, where from the moment I woke up that morning, I just knew we were going to win. David Villa's vaguely annoying goal only made the comeback even better. I don't think I could choose my favourite moment, but one that will stay with me forever was being at the San Siro in 2008 when we beat AC Milan 2-0. The lashing rain, the seats so high we might as well have been on the moon, the stinky toilets with the menacingly wet floor, then the goals. There were two men sitting in front of us. At the beginning of the match, they were drunk. Really drunk. So drunk. Pressing their noses up against the partition and making ugly faces at the home fans drunk. By half-time they'd calmed down a bit. They sat, heads in hands, the tension clearly making their beered-up brains heavier. When the full-time whistle came, with everyone else jumping up and down hugging, one turned to the other, tears on his face, and said, 'If I never see another game of football, I will still die a happy man'.

If you could bottle that feeling of an unexpected win, minus the inevitable hangover, it would be the bottle you keep for a really special occasion that never seems to come along. I knew exactly how he felt, aside from the man part. I cry all the time in matches. My sister is almost as much of a football wimp. I cry when it's good, I cry when it's bad. I cried when we were beaten by Barcelona in the Champions League final and I cried when we beat Liverpool 1-0 at home last year. It's pathetic, but it's football. There are so many people in the world who don't care for it. They look down their noses at it as being overpaid, morally bankrupt, beneath good society. Increasingly, they're quite right. But it doesn't stop me from pitying them, in the knowledge they'll never have a chance to feel what it is to be a passionate football supporter. There are some amazing writers on the sport, of both professional and amateur works, who manage to possess an incredible knowledge of the game without ever pledging allegiance to a single individual team. It's impressive, and a bit weird. I also know a lot of people who support multiple teams. That's their choice and good on them for actually managing to find the time and patience to dedicate to so much football. There is simply no way I could handle the stress of more than one. Besides, we are by far the greatest team the world has ever seen so who needs anyone else?

I have one mum, one dad, and one sister. And then I have the Arsenal. I only became aware I had him at the age of six or seven. He's a total problem child, who gives me sleepless nights and lost voices and stress headaches. Other people really dislike him, and really enjoy kicking him when he's down. I can complain about him as much as I like, but anyone else trying it will get an earful at best, and a bruise at worst. When he's bad he's annoying, but when he's good he makes the world the best it can possibly be. Friends, jobs, boyfriends and homes will come and go, but the Arsenal will always be there, whether he's being mean or magnificent.

And that, I think, is family.

Sian Ranscombe has been writing her blog 'From A Girl Who Loves The Gunners' since March 2010. Her favourite on the current team varies between Bacary Sagna and Thomas Vermaelen, depending on who is less injured at the time.

12

ARSENE WENGER AND TACTICS

MICHAEL COX

"The team talk was at 12:55pm and lasted just five minutes while Arsene named the team. No-one was really too surprised or too disappointed; we had seen the way it was shaping up in training during the week. Chris Wreh, rather than a fit-again Ian Wright, was always going to be Dennis Bergkamp's replacement. At 1:05pm we left. Not once had we discussed Newcastle. We were confident enough that if we played well, we wouldn't need to worry about them."

Tony Adams in his autobiography, Addicted, on the 1998 FA Cup final preparations.

There lies Arsene Wenger's greatest strength when trophies are won, and arguably his most obvious weakness when

Arsenal lose a big game. He is not inherently a tactician – he's not a chalkboard man, not likely to win games based upon an unusual formation decision or a clever, game-changing substitution. He has an overarching ideology rather than a series of smaller policies, and Adams' final line typifies that.

THE DEFINITION OF TACTICS

It depends what you consider 'tactics'. Brian Clough only ever used the word to refer to how he would go about stopping the opposition. In other words, nothing natural or positive his side did was a 'tactic', and so tactic became a dirty word, perhaps a predecessor to 'anti-football'. If you send your side out for a Cup Final without mentioning the opposition, by Clough's definition, you do not have any tactics. That example from 1998 appears to be extreme, even for Wenger. At that point, the approach was probably justified – Arsenal had won the league, were the best team in the country, and could afford to go out, do their thing and be confident of taking the game to the opposition. It worked rather well. Besides, in that age, English games simply weren't as tactical as they are now: it was 4-4-2 against 4-4-2. Games were based around physicality and technical quality rather than tactical acumen; and individual battles were more important than a clash of systems.

It is debatable whether such an approach is workable in the modern era, yet Wenger's attitude seems to have remained more or less unchanged. On the way to winning the World Cup in 2010, Cesc Fabregas compared preparations at Spain with pre-match discussions at Arsenal. "Here (with Spain) they give us more information, definitely. At Arsenal we don't really look at anything from the other team, we look at ourselves, and that's it." It is amazing, and yet not surprising to anyone who has followed Arsenal over the past 15 years. In recent years the side has struggled against managers like Jose Mourinho and Sir Alex Ferguson, who both adapt their team to the conditions of the game. Against lower sides, Arsenal always appear surprised when they come up against a team who 'parks the bus'. There's rarely an obvious approach to exploit weaknesses in the opposition. Arsenal essentially play the same way from game to game, and sometimes it has catastrophic results – most obviously in the August 2011 defeat by Manchester United, a barely believable scoreline of 8-2.

"Let me put it in perspective," began Paul Merson, a pundit on Sky for that humiliating defeat. "There'll be a lot lesser teams with much less talent than Arsenal who will come to Old Trafford this season, and make it twice as difficult (for United). You've got to have tactics. You can't just have a plan A; you've got to have a plan B. Don't put those kind of players on the pitch as lambs to the slaughter… you can't keep on putting teams out and saying 'play the Arsenal way' – it's not good enough."

PLAN B

Ah, the old plan B. In a way, it's nice to hear it in a different context; usually it's been used to refer to what Arsenal rarely had: that penalty box striker who could allow a more direct game. Here, of course, it is used in a broader sense, but it's still the idea that Arsenal can only play one way. For the most part, this is true. Except for one thing – two things, in fact. The last two occasions Arsenal can count as achievements – winning the FA Cup final in 2005, and getting to the European Cup final of 2006 – came when Arsenal played football that was much more defensive than usual. Wenger significantly altered his tactics to become a reactive side, one that played 4-5-1 and defended deep, before countering. On the European run of 2006, Arsenal kept ten clean sheets in a row against the likes of Ajax, Juventus, Real Madrid and Villarreal. Admittedly, it meant a slightly more negative style of football, the second leg of each knockout tie finished 0-0. But for that season, Arsenal combined resilience and organisation at the back with real quality going forward. No-one was complaining about the football not being attacking enough when Robert Pires slipped Cesc Fabregas in at home to Juventus, or when Thierry Henry scored his brilliant solo goal away in the Bernabeu.

The FA Cup final success was, in truth, something of a fluke. United recorded 20 shots to Arsenal's five; eight on target to Arsenal's one: one, in 120 minutes. That quite clearly wasn't playing 'the Arsenal way', but the trophy was in the bag. The frustration, then is, why couldn't Wenger have shown a little more pragmatism during other key moments? Arsenal have missed out on trophies when they became too predictable, too easy to play against. Often, it has been against much weaker opposition. The 2004 Champions League quarter-final defeat to Chelsea stands out as a missed opportunity, a time when Arsenal could have set up more intelligently over the two legs, but eventually went out to an inferior team. The 2011 Carling Cup final defeat was Arsenal at their worst: horrendously predictable and easy to play against. Birmingham were an awful team, relegated at the end of the season; yet Alex McLeish tactically out-thought Wenger, with Arsenal content to play their usual brand of football. Wenger is the manager that every fan wants to be in control of their club long-term, but arguably not the man to win individual contests.

PLAN A?

But if we're going on about plan B, what was plan A? After all, we can't take Clough's view on tactics as gospel. Rinus Michels, the legendary father of Total Football at Ajax, thought of tactics as everything on the pitch. If we take this view of tactics, Wenger is a genius. He is unashamedly a romantic, insisting upon open, attacking football. "I believe the target of anything in life should be to do it so well that it becomes an art," he told Martin Samuel of the Daily Mail. "When you read some books they are fantastic, the writer touches something in you that you know you would not have brought out of yourself. He makes you discover something interesting in your life. If you are living like an animal, what is the point of living? What makes daily life interesting is that we try to transform it to something that is close to art. And football is like that."

It's astonishing that Wenger has managed to instil this as such a core principle at a club like Arsenal, a club who spent the years before Wenger arrived being mocked for their awful football. "Really, Arsenal were terrible," says Nick Hornby, in David Winner's book 'Those Feet'. "It was as bad as it ever got just before George Graham got sacked." That was 1995. Three years later Arsenal were winning the league in the most fabulous way possible, with two of the old guard, Steve Bould and Tony Adams, combining for the brilliant clinching goal at home to Everton.

Wenger's 'art' was never likely to be questioned when Arsenal were winning the league, but probably his greatest achievement is that he managed to sustain support amongst the vast majority of Arsenal fans when things were going poorly, partly because of the style of play. To justify poor results because of the way the poor results were achieved is, in simple terms, extraordinarily cheeky. It is roughly equivalent to a used car salesman maintaining the full support of his boss, despite never selling any cars, because he turned up for work every day dressed immaculately. "If asked you who was the best team in the world you would say Brazil," Wenger said in 2009. "And do they play good football? Yes. Which club won everything last year? Barcelona. Good football."

He's got a point; 'style' and 'results' are not mutually exclusive, but the sides he mentioned were managed by men, (Dunga and Pep Guardiola), who were both tactical obsessives. It's probably easier for a pure tactician to play attractive football than it is for a beautiful football advocate to become a tactical master.

DEVELOPMENT OF WENGERISM

That's not to say that Arsenal have had no shape or system. Wenger's sides have never been like the mid-2000s Real Madrid Galacticos, for example. The system used has always seemed to be a by-product of the players on offer, however. Studying Wenger's formations over the years isn't particularly enlightening, though it's interesting to review something he told Gianluca Vialli back in 2006. "I think 4-4-2 is simply the most rational formation in most cases," he said. "In fact, it's the essence of reason. With a 4-4-2, 60% of your players are covering 60% of the space."

The real progression of his tactics has not been about static formations; it has been about the method of attack. When he first arrived, Arsenal were based around playing on the counter-attack. Marc Overmars was flying down the left; Ian Wright and then Nicolas Anelka were providing pace over the top, whilst Ray Parlour had a great turn of speed on the right. Even Bergkamp wasn't slow. In fact, when Arsenal did physical tests of their players in the 2003/04 season, at 34, Bergkamp was the third-quickest player at the club, behind Thierry Henry and Jermaine Pennant. That's from a start line featuring the likes of Ashley Cole, Robert Pires and Sylvain Wiltord.

Think back to the three games that clinched titles for Wenger, and all three conjure up memories of goals on the break. Overmars was the key man in the early days, with the two goals he scored in the aforementioned 4-0 win over Everton – picking up the ball to feet in midfield, and simply roaring past the opposition on his way to goal. Freddie Ljungberg darting through the Manchester United defence to set up a rebound for Wiltord in 2002 was another example, as was Patrick Vieira's imperious stride through the Tottenham defence to slide in the opener at White Hart Lane in 2004. The main man throughout the middle part of Wenger's time in charge was Thierry Henry, the personification of intelligent counter-attacking. In the same way Johan Cruyff typified Dutch total football, and Xavi Hernandez is the main man in Barcelona's tiki-taka, Henry was a counter-attacking virtuoso.

At some point, possibly linked to Henry's departure, a predominantly counter-attacking approach seemed to be ditched, and Arsenal became ball hoarders. The likes of Alexander Hleb, Tomas Rosicky, Samir Nasri and Andrei Arshavin arrived, all looking to come inside from wide positions and pass their way through the opposition defence. Too often moves were slow and too easy to defend against, with a narrow opposition playing deep and narrow, making it impossible for Arsenal to use pace over or through the defence. During this time, Arsenal were allowed to play pretty, but fruitless, football and get away with it, perhaps under Wenger's 'art' comfort blanket. Ironically, that type of football was perfect for the opposition to counter-attack themselves, with Manchester United doing this particularly successfully at the Emirates. Cristiano Ronaldo's goal in 2009 and Wayne Rooney's in 2010 on the break were superb footballing goals. Arsenal seem to have lost the ability to score like that. Hleb, an unquestionably talented footballer, epitomised the approach. Despite his promise he never became a truly effective player in the final third, and his rate of goals and assists was derisory compared to Robert Pires or Freddie Ljungberg. He often dribbled for 40 yards, before turning back and playing a simple ball when the killer pass was on. He, Rosicky and Arshavin now seem much less direct than when they arrived at the club. Strangely, imagine a pitch from above, and their movements are probably identical to that of Pires and Ljungberg – start on the flanks, cut inside to the centre. But those two did so when the rest of the side played at speed, and they broke past the defence.

These days the wide players drift to the centre obviously, rather than turn up there unannounced.

It all just seems too slow, and Arsenal fans' continued, admirable patience with Theo Walcott is surely not just because he seems like a nice young chap, but because he offers that raw pace and a chance to break quickly. His assist for Emmanuel Adebayor at Anfield in 2008 was old school Arsenal, and he has done similar on a few occasions since. The criticism he receives in some quarters is extremely harsh, but even if you do believe that he has 'no footballing brain', so be it. Arsenal have had plenty of players with good football brains; having one with pure pace is a welcome relief.

The summer of 2011 might turn out to be a move back to the directness of early Wenger. With two passers, Cesc Fabregas and Samir Nasri, departing the club and Gervinho coming in, it points to more of a 'vertical' game when in possession, something Arsenal desperately need. There are plenty of other variables, but Wenger's trophies have come when Arsenal were more counter-attack-based and slightly less possession-orientated, although a combination of both is always ideal.

CONCLUSION

All this is intended as a critique rather than a criticism of Wenger. As mentioned previously, his achievement in shifting the goalposts of what constitutes 'success' is remarkable.

That said, in the grand scheme of things, seven trophies in 15 years seems low for such a wonderful manager who will certainly go down as a club legend – especially in an era when trophies are won almost exclusively by the top four, of which Arsenal have remained a part of since Wenger's arrival. The truth is that 'tactics' are a way to get around not being the better team on paper. Arsenal have only won trophies when they've been the best team – the one exception being the 2005 FA Cup final. The title should have been won in 2003 and the Champions League seemed Arsenal's before the exit to Chelsea in 2004. The UEFA Cup final defeat in 2000 to an inferior Galatasaray still rankles, whilst the FA Cup of 2001 and Carling Cup of 2011 were lost late on, but again, to weaker sides. That is five separate extra trophies should have won based on pure talent, but other sides maximised their resources and overcame Wenger's side. We are left to conclude then that Wenger is a great legacy builder, an astute economist, a revolutionary physiologist, an intelligent communicator, a good man manager and an admirable footballing philosopher – but probably not a great tactician.

Michael Cox writes tactics blog Zonal Marking, as well as weekly columns for the Guardian, ESPN and FourFourTwo.com

13

OUR PRIVATE GARDEN

TIM BOSTELLE

CHARLTON – 18.03.2006

You see your first live Arsenal match when you are 35 years old.

Maybe circumstances in life contrived to prevent you from going; illness, that time you lost your job right before you were going to make the trip, your ex-wife refusing you the luxury, it was always something. Maybe you're one of those people who always loved Arsenal but lived somewhere far away and you happen to suffer a Bergkamp-like hatred of flying. Or maybe you're one of those people who publicly talk about how much they loathe sports but secretly always rooted for Arsenal and finally decided to make the plunge. Whatever it is, you find yourself at Highbury on 18 March 2006, nursing a

St. Patrick's Day-sized hangover, and an hour early for Arsenal v. Charlton.

You wander around in the belly of Highbury wondering what you can get from the vendors that will cure this hangover. The burgers on Avenell road have piqued your appetite as they fill the air with the smell of grilled onions and charred meat but you pass them by as possibly unsanitary. Instead, you choose the sanitized offerings inside Highbury herself and get a flat, iceless, Coke and something that is advertised as a pie. As you sip the Coke and poke at the pie, you decide that diarrhea from a burger on Avenell road might be preferable to this.

The West Lower concourse is, well, minimalist is a nice way of putting it. After a few minutes of looking at some posters and a few videos on the retrofitted televisions you decide that you might as well find your seat. You start the climb from the concourse to the stands and it strikes you how well worn the stairs are here. Deep grooves have been left from the millions of footsteps that tread this path before. And just as you start to imagine the first family that made this same walk back in 1913, you see over the top of the last stair and the most beautiful green field you have ever seen fills your eyes.

It's impossible to stop from letting out a gasp. The sky is perfectly blue. The stands are perfectly red, the art deco buildings perfectly off-white. There's the Herbert Chapman Arsenal symbol. The clock. Your mind races from one object to the other. But it's the pitch that draws you back. When God created the colour green he did so by planting a field in Highbury and a stadium must have sprung up around that, with Archibald Leitch declaring, "Here would be a fine place to play football."

Why had you waited so long for this? Forgetting the lethargy from your hangover, now you greedily rush toward the pitch. Row after row fades behind you until you find your seat. It's perfect: slightly off centre, close to the pitch, with no obstructions. The minutes now fly by as you stand there drinking in the history all around you.

A Pires goal snaps you out of your stupor in the 13th minute. The crowd erupts as Henry takes a pass from Hleb, plays a give-and-go with Adebayor and slots it across for Bobby to put away easily. "One-nil to the Arsenal," sweeps through the crowd and you join in, sheepishly, not wanting to be found out as the interloper. Adebayor gets the second after a poor defensive clearance sets him free on goal and Hleb puts away the third after half-time to round off the day. This is love. Your friends who don't watch football won't understand. Your friends who do watch football, but have never been to see a game, won't understand. This is suddenly one of the top experiences in your life. Better than your first kiss (that was two teenagers blindly groping in the basement). Better than your first love (because Arsenal hadn't broken your heart yet). You walk out into the sunshine knowing that Arsenal will always be there for you. If you yell at Arsenal she wont leave you. If you treat Arsenal badly she won't cheat on you with another. Win or lose, Arsenal will never break your heart.

SUNDERLAND – 21.02.2009

Every relationship reaches a point where you can finish each other's sentences. Maybe it's the familiarity of the rhythm of her speech or maybe there is some collective unconscious that two people share after years of being together. Whatever the cause, you are now at this point in your love affair with Arsenal. The stories that you share with Arsenal feel nearly as well worn as those Highbury steps that first led you down this path. "The Emirates had to be built," you hear yourself saying, "in order to compete with the financial powers of Chelsea." Adrian sips his beer and nods approvingly at this. "Besides which," you continue, "Arsenal generate more in gate receipts than almost any other team in the world, the loans are at an incredibly manageable rate and it won't be long now before Highbury is rebuilt and the club recover the money from that investment."

You feel comfortable saying all this; it feels like the truth. It will only be a matter of time before Abramovich calls in all those loans we found out he put on the Chelsea's books or the banks call in the debts at Man United and Liverpool, and as soon as those three clubs collapse under the weight of their 'financial doping' the distorting effect of their funny money in the transfer market will be nothing more than a footnote in football history.

You can't help but chuckle as you sip your beer. Adrian looks at you a bit strangely. The arguments are very familiar but you've crossed the line from casual supporter to fervent believer and you both know it. After a few sips of beer in silence you finally admit that it would be highly unlikely that a rich investor would turn down the opportunity to buy Manchester United.

"Another pint?" he asks. "No, you know I like to get to the stadium early."

It's been your tradition since Highbury to get to the stadium as early as possible and hit the stores. You only go once a year so you like to drink in the whole experience. It's a beautiful day, the sun is shining, and you have this really great feeling that everything is going to go well. When choosing matches to attend you look at the fixtures that seem most likely to produce a win. With all the money it costs to travel, you don't want to risk the insult of a loss, so you pick teams that seem reasonable for Arsenal to beat. This year, though, you could only go to see Sunderland. Unfortunately, Sunderland is always a tough match because Steve Bruce likes to keep his teams well disciplined and likes to hit Arsenal with a quick counter. But we have a secret weapon; the eagerly awaited unveiling of Arsene Wenger's latest multi-million pound signing; Andrei Arshavin, is rumoured to be playing today.

Everyone at the Arsenal store is in a buoyant mood, milling about and festooning each other with Arsenal swag. As you are having Eduardo's name pressed into your shirt you ask the kid behind the counter when the last time he pressed an Eboue shirt? He laughs and says it was probably the time Eboue came in and bought a bunch of shirts with his own name on them. Emirates stadium is magnificent in its efficiency. Unlike the crowded old hallways of Highbury, the wide concourses at the Emirates allow people to move about freely from food stand to food stand. Sure, a line still forms for the urinal at half time and men stinking of hot piss and beer still stand impatiently in line to empty their bladders but filling those bladders is amazingly efficient. There are now dozens of beer stands all with several open lines each with its very own bored-looking cashier just waiting to serve you a nice cold beer or a £5 hot dog.

When Arshavin's name is announced as a starter there is a huge roar from the crowd: the man who has come to save our season has finally arrived. Grinning from ear to ear you eagerly join in the chant of "There's Only One Arsene Wenger," and it helps push back that nagging feeling that Arsenal are fifth in the table and things are looking grim. The match is on, the sun is out in February, and Arsenal are going to wipe out the memory of two consecutive nil-nil draws. Unfortunately, you later learn, kick-off was the happiest part of the match.

The crowd is buzzing and Arshavin looks fantastic right off the bat but from there on in it's all downhill. The first half moves from buzzing anticipation to utter frustration: Bendtner squanders a chance, Arshavin misses two, and even van Persie misses a shot. The team is moving the ball well but struggling in the final third, and fan unrest starts to build. At first it is directed at the ref, then towards the Sunderland players, and supporters; finally, by the end of the match, our own players.

If the first-half is bad, the second is immeasurably worse. The entire second-half is played at the other end of the pitch. And whether it is the booze or the boredom, the two guys from Ireland in front of you are passed out and sleeping quite peacefully. Sunderland have literally put Arsenal to sleep. Toward the end, Sunderland supporters are cheering every Arsenal pass with an "Olé!" and shushing us incessantly. Every part of your body wants so badly for Arsenal to score so that you can turn to the Sunderland fans and shush them right back. It doesn't happen.

At the very end of the match a couple Arsenal fans and at least one Sunderland fan are ejected for giving each other the finger and yelling obscenities. This is the most excitement you feel for 80 minutes. The full time whistle blows and you stand in line waiting to shuffle out of the stadium. You steal a glance at the Sunderland supporters who are dancing, their arms raised in the air and fists pumping in a pantomime of what they would do if they could ever win the league. Instead it's just a nil-nil jig.

Looking down at the steps you realize you'd never been to a match where Arsenal failed to win, much less one where they failed to score. It's a raw feeling; Arsenal are 6 points behind Villa and Sunderland supporters are dancing a jig on our grave. In a daze you leave the stadium and wander the wrong way back to the tube station. As you stroll down Avenell Road, the East Stand draws you in. If you squint you can just see through the scaffolding's cover and note that backhoes litter the old pitch. Highbury, the place where you fell in love with the Arsenal is being rebuilt as apartments for the wealthy. So that we have money to compete with Chelsea and Man U, you remind yourself.

BIRMINGHAM CITY – 27.02.2011

You join the main throng of Gooners leaving Wembley. Out of what must now be nervous habit, you look down at the steps. Wembley's steps are fresher than Emirates Stadium you notice. You're shocked out of contemplation when a man throws his programme so hard it seems as if it might break the chair in front of him. Another man slams his fist against the same chairs and you wonder if he broke his hand. The boy who had been in front of you for the full 90 minutes is being carried by his father, tears sting his eyes as he looks up to the score board before quickly burying his head back into his father's shoulders.

The day starts perfectly. You seem to have a knack for picking beautiful days to watch Arsenal and this is no different. A beautiful day; Arsenal playing Birmingham in their first cup-final since the disaster against Chelsea and there's a feeling of optimism in the air. You have sun block on, your Bergkamp shirt from the 2006 season, and you feel… well, you feel invincible. The Jubilee Line carriage you're in has just five men in Arsenal shirts and one boy. There's a lot of nervous laughter as both groups circle round each other and make chit-chat. Strangely, no one is talking about the game ahead. There are no predictions of first goal scorer, or final score. Instead they focus on small things going on in their lives. Whenever the occasional Birmingham supporter boards the train they smile at us politely and take a seat. They all look relaxed and ready for the day out; to a man we look nervous and excited.

The night before the match you go out with some friends for drinks and as the night wears on you notice some Birmingham supporters at the bar. One fellow must have had his fill of drinks because he's talking very loudly to his friend about the game the next day. "I hate the arrogance of these Arsenal pricks," he projects for all to hear. "They act so confident that they are going to win but ask one of them this: 'Give me 50 to 1 odds and I'll put a tenner on it,' and watch their confidence fade." The real odds are Birmingham 7-1 which is

a far more realistic prospect than 50-1 but despite the hyperbole the point is decent enough: the thought that Arsenal
would lose the next day makes you and your friends laugh.

Wembley has a single main walkway to and from the stadium ringed by various carts of foods you decide no person
should eat. The sun is gone and the rain is pissing down
now. Arsenal supporters mingle with Birmingham supporters as we all make our way down the promenade to
Wembley proper. Red flags, blue flags, and chequered jester's hats festoon both sets of fans. Someone near you starts
singing, "Ooh to, Ooh to be, Ooh to be a GOONAH."
Dozens around him join in forming a small chorus of
Arsenal fans. A group of Birmingham supporters with
blue and white jester's hats walk past the chorus and smile.
Five folks parked next to a burger van are keeping dry by
waving a giant Arsenal flag over their heads, singing "Na
na na na na na na na na na na nasiri, na na nasiriii!" The
Birmingham supporters remain silent, while us Gooners
are whooping it up. It's as if we are already celebrating.

"WHY CAN'T WE DEFEND A SIMPLE
HEADER???" The action happens so quickly and your
angle is so acute that you look up to the 'Jumbotron' to
see Zigic score the opener. In real time the goal looks like
something Birmingham had drawn up on the training
ground. Arsenal are vulnerable, more so than any other
team, to the second header. So when we get to the first
header we don't clear our lines well and teams will simply

play it back in and keep us under pressure. But this header was special: we've all seen teams play a long corner, head it back across, and while our defenders are chasing ghosts, it's a free for the opposition's big man.

As soon as the ball ripples the opposition net we jump in joy. Pure jubilation spreads like wildfire through our end of the stadium. The Arsenal fans sing again now. "We love you Arsenal", is the chant of the moment. The boy in front of you, draped in an Arsenal flag like a superhero's cape, is in his father's arms, fat tears rolling down his cheeks. Tears of joy; relief, anguish, and worst of all, tears of belief. Robin van Persie scores the equalizer and there is suddenly real belief in both the fans and the players. The other end of the stadium simultaneously sits on their hands. There is still a whole second half to play but the flags are put away and as Arsenal attack the Birmingham goal relentlessly they seem resolved that the loss is coming.

The sound of Martins' goal reaches our end of the stadium like a sonic boom. We watch the collision of Koscielny and Szczesny, see the net ripple. You look over at the linesman in desperation but he's not waving his flag. Mike Dean signals a goal; the sound of Birmingham fans celebrating the winner washes over us. Our end of the stadium is knocked back a bit. There is time left on the clock but we know that it is over: the singing is done, and we look around at each other helpless to do anything but stand there and wallow in frustration.

As we approach the first of several ramps out of Wembley people voice that frustration. "If anyone here thinks Bendtner is a striker raise your hand." No one replies. "Why can't we just buy a £20m centre-half and defend set pieces?" says another. On it goes; outbursts of anger like little firecrackers erupting all over the crowd.

Then someone starts to sing in sotto voce "Number 1 is Perry Groves… Number 2 is Perry Groves… Number 3 is Perry Groves…" and one by one, others join. After that song dies down, the next song picks up "There's only one Tony Adams." Clearly Gooners want those old days back. And who can blame them? Here was the chance to get Arsenal back on a winning track and to prove the Emirates project could pay dividends in the trophy cabinet. But the dream slipped away into the dark, cold, night.

The next day, you decide you have enough time before heading home to stop at Highbury and see what the club has done to the old Lady. It's been a year, but Arsenal station is still the same: the same cattle-walk to allow people who aren't going to a game to pass the crowds quickly; the same North London row houses right outside the station. Even the "Allez Arsenal" that you first noticed three years ago is still scrawled into the concrete as you approach the East stand.

You have seen all the brochures and know what Highbury is being redesigned into, but the full shock of the gleaming condos and imperious black gate is unexpected.

You stand outside the gate and look inside, it dawns on you that you'll never set foot in there again. You'll never walk up those old stairs ever again. The old songs sung by the crowds will never echo from stand to stand. The ground where you and countless others fell in love with Arsenal has been fenced off and made into a rich man's private garden.

Tim Bostelle is paid to do something other than write about Arsenal at 7amkickoff.com but he finds a way to do it every day regardless.

14

ARSENAL'S STANDING IN THE MODERN GAME

STUART STRATFORD

As football changes, the standing of a club in the modern game becomes more obscured. There is a proliferation of information with the global, and seemingly endless, reach of the Internet. Any club can be deemed to be the biggest in the world using one yardstick or another. Life was not always this complicated. Rewind a century and Arsenal were on the cusp of "negotiating" their way into English football's top flight, a place they still occupy. The arrival of Herbert Chapman would take the club to another level altogether.

By the time the 1930's had finished and the world was at war, Arsenal had become The Establishment Club. The rise had been prolific. The club were crowned Champions in 1953 for the seventh time, then a record. As well as the titles, there were three victorious FA Cup Finals. Not bad for a club whose first major honour came with a 2-0 victory over Huddersfield Town in the 1930 FA Cup final. Since those times, success and failure have been equal bedfellows. If the period 1955 – 1967 was the nadir, the reign of Arsène Wenger has been the peak. In between, glory and fallow periods were close cousins. Football is a cyclical sport; few other clubs have a history as illustrious or which proves that as emphatically as Arsenal's.

Before the 1950's, it was easy to measure a club's standing in the game. Parochial administrators ensured that their personal fiefdoms were unchallenged and uncomplicated by journeys to foreign shores, save for pre-season tours. How good was your team? Where did they finish in the league last season? Did they win the FA Cup? How many times have they won both competitions? Answer those questions and you found out how 'big' your club was.

But football is changing. Records created have become ghosts of a game that has taken to discarding the past with relative ease and a total lack of conscience. Many records have been created in the club's 125 year existence. Some, such as The Invincibles, still stand, as does the near century tenure in the top-flight of English football. Others, such as becoming the first team to win 7 league titles back in 1950s, have been surpassed and ground into the dust of football's past.

The modern game is light years away from its ancestors. Money swirls in and out of the game, caught in a typhoon of greed and glory. The past is suppressed and consigned to obscure satellite channels, packaged in highlights bundles for the midnight hour. Football's face has been surgically altered and botoxed beyond recognition. And where does this leave Arsenal?

Boundaries are being wiped away. The Internet means that fans in geographically disparate locations can chat as easily about the match as our forefathers did in the pub following the final whistle. As club sides go, Arsenal has one of the most internet-active sets of supporters. It is difficult to quantify but this experience makes them one of the biggest clubs in the world by that measure. If this is the case, why is the media perception so different? Why are Arsenal treated as poor relations to other clubs, including those who make their debuts in the Champions League this season.

Investment is happening on a global scale. The European leagues, traditionally considered the biggest, are not necessarily the richest. Super clubs are emerging from the former Russian states; oligarchs invest vast sums for players in order to chase Champions League glory. The most startling example is at Russian club, Anzhi Makhachkala, who signed Samuel Eto'o on a deal rumoured to be worth £250k per week after tax, on top of a £22m fee to Internazionale. Perhaps the biggest change is coming with the arrival of Middle Eastern money. Beneficiaries include Paris St Germain and Malaga, neither of whom are reluctant to flash the new found cash. For years the Parisians lost their best players to others, now they enjoy the role reversal. Malaga has spent heavily in an attempt to gate-crash the top table in Spain. They will find little room with Barcelona and Real Madrid unwilling to share space. Indeed, with so few challengers they have made it all but impossible for anyone to win the title such is their dominance of revenues.

The biggest change is at Manchester City. Having invested heavily in previous summers, they have moved up another level with money and quality of players bought. Already targeted by UEFA under the Financial Fair Play regulations (FFP) for their sponsorship deal, City need to increase their revenues to cover ever-increasing costs. Already this summer they found it hard to dispose of players, doing loan deals with Tottenham and others to cut their playing staff. These clubs offer the biggest threat to the status quo. As they spend more on fees and wages, traditionally run clubs are marginalised in the transfer market. No longer is the solution to slowly build a squad, promoting youth with a mix of older heads. The Super Clubs want it all and they want it now, purchasing their way to silverware as quickly as they can. The FFP rules will counter some of the excesses, but not all of them as clubs become more commercially aware, exploiting their brands in the global marketplace.

Arsenal has not taken advantage of this. Tied into sponsorship deals that helped to build their new stadium,

the club's commercial revenues are found badly wanting when compared to their domestic and international
rivals. Negotiations have not brought forth solutions,
the club reluctant to follow Chelsea's lead in paying off
previous sponsors to negotiate more commercially advan-
tageous deals. To put Arsenal's position into perspective,
Manchester United's recent sponsorship deal with DHL
for their training kit compares more than favourably with
Arsenal's for their first XI shirts. Summer 2011 was the first
time in forty years that the club had ventured to the Far
East for a tour, but two matches played in Asia hardly constitutes a massive commitment. Dipping their toes in is fine
but rivals such as United and Chelsea exploited these mar-
kets long ago, moving onto the United States of America
for their pre-season tours. Having an American billionaire
owner, Arsenal will presumably follow that path. Arsène
Wenger's opposition to such matters will be considered but
ultimately ignored in the pursuit of financial enhancement.
Arsenal needs it. Wenger admits that once the bigger clubs
come into the process, Arsenal will always lose out in a bid-
ding war for either transfer fees or wages. This suggests that
in the modern game, Arsenal's business model is wrong.

How do they alter it? Alisher Usmanov makes the
right noises publicly but finds little support for his desire
to invest, particularly as he seems more concerned with
dividends. The Uzbek wants us to believe he would invest
heavily on the playing side but it is easy to say these things

when you know there is little or no chance of your offer being taken. However, even the biggest clubs around the world have hit financial trouble with the traditional football model. Barcelona had severe cash flow problems at the end of the 2010/11 season whilst the debt incurred by the Glazers in purchasing Manchester United has necessitated them floating part of the club on the Singapore Stock Exchange. By comparison, Arsenal remains financially one of the most valuable clubs in the world; the self-sustaining model employed by the club shows its worth in various lists compiled by both Deloittes and Forbes. The Emirates Stadium has increased match-day revenue, enabling higher wages to be paid amongst the squad (although wages paid at Arsenal are easily and willingly trumped by Chelsea and both Mancunian clubs). Can they compete at the highest level continually when faced with those whose spending power far outweighs their own? The answer to that is quite simple: they must. It is a trite observation but true nonetheless. Clubs such as Arsenal competing with those who utilise what Wenger calls 'financial doping' are necessary for the good of the game. If Arsenal fail and no-one else steps forward to take their place, money has won. Michel Platini might worry that overt corruption will ruin the professional game, the imbalance caused by huge investments from owners or bankers, covertly corrupts football. This is not to cast Arsenal as a White Knight. They are not fighting any such battle for the good of the game, simply for the good of Arsenal Football Club. It is the corner into which they have been painted. Football is such a fluid game on and off the pitch, that this year's financial champions may be next year's Sugar Daddy plaything.

This year saw a change in the perception of Arsenal. Previous years had seen the club tipped to be the one of the 'Big Four' who dropped out of contention. Liverpool filled that gap instead, the season after finishing runners-up. Arsenal launched a title challenge in 2010/11 that eventually withered away into a struggle for fourth place. The departures of Cesc Fabregas and Samir Nasri have been seen as cataclysmic for the club. If you strip away the hyperbole, losing two key players is bound to impact any team. Wenger, though, has negatively influenced opinion on this matter. Whilst not setting the agenda, he did nothing to diffuse the situation. Speaking on the club's Asian tour, he observed, "Imagine the worst situation – we lose Fabregas and Nasri – you cannot convince people you are ambitious after that ... I believe for us it is important that the message we give out – for example you see about Fabregas leaving, Nasri leaving – if you give that message out you cannot pretend you are a big club. Because a big club first of all holds onto its big players and gives a message out to all the other big clubs that they just cannot come in and take [players] away from you."

It is the language of football, the self-aggrandisement of the sport. The words have come back to haunt him on more than one occasion, gleefully thrown back in his face by his critics. It begs the question, can Arsenal be considered a big club if they cannot hold onto their best players? The issue is clouded by the context of the sales. Fabregas was returning home, to a former club, a club he supports and had done since he was a child. In that instance, is it a diminution of Arsenal's status to sell the player, particularly since his new employers are considered to be one of the best club sides in football's history?

In my opinion, it is the sale of Nasri that highlights the problems Arsenal face most. The player had all but agreed a deal to extend his contract with Arsenal. Something happened at the start of the 2010/11 season that put the matter on ice, the suspicion is that his agent had contact with other clubs and the player's head was turned by the money on offer elsewhere. The wages he plumped for at Man City were £75k more than Arsenal offered and was willing to pay. City had the need and economic means to pay the substantial sum, showing that they were in a hurry to snap up any talent that became available in their avaricious pursuit of silverware, emphasising the wealth gap created.

So, does this signal a lack of ambition? Nasri has not been backwards in stating that this is so, criticising the board – not Wenger though – for failing to back the manager in the transfer market. With any media interview caution must be applied but if players believe the club lacks ambition, surely there is something in what Nasri says? Again context comes into play. The Frenchman's last days at the club were rife with acrimony; many supporters maligned him as treacherous and greedy. Nasri hit back at his critics, feeding prejudices, while trying to portray himself in a more favourable light.

Losing key players, no matter the reason, suggests the club are not achieving their targets. Were Arsenal Champions of England, or Europe, on a regular basis, would Fabregas have been so eager to leave? It's hard to prove but had Arsenal achieved silverware in the previous seasons it would certainly have made his decision more difficult. And therein lies the crux of the matter. For all of these reasons Arsenal can be considered a big club, a crucial one contradicts the argument: trophies; or to be more precise, the lack of them in recent seasons. Since winning the FA Cup in 2005, Arsenal lost in the Champions League final as well as two Carling Cup finals. Defeats have also come at the semi-final stage of the Champions League and both domestic cups. Always the bridesmaid: never the bride.

Does this matter in the context of Arsenal and the modern game? It does, simply because of the vicious circle that exists at the top level of professional football. To attract the best players, you must win silverware. If you don't, the best players will be reluctant to join. It highlights the vacuous nature of many footballers that they leave clubs bemoaning the lack of silverware without the slightest hint of taking personal responsibility for their part in that failure. Arsenal remains one of the game's biggest clubs but it is a position increasingly under threat. No matter what the finances might say, it is honours that matter more. There is little point in being rich and mediocre. The club's challenge over the coming years will be building a winning squad, one that can compete with wealthier clubs on a regular basis, and one that can sustain its place amongst football's elite.

Stuart Stratford is the author of Arsenal blog, A Cultured Left Foot

15

WEMBLEY. BASTARD WEMBLEY

TIM CLARK

Wembley. Bastard Wembley. For some, it must be a Champagne-splashed coliseum of pleasure, forever ringing to the sound of 'Campeones!', fireworks, and Laura Wright lustily belting out the National Anthem. Not for me. For me it's the kind of shithole that gives shitholes a bad name: an ugly, rain-blasted concrete mausoleum. It is the place where my Carling Cup dream crawled to die.

Yes, that's right: dream.

Okay, look, I know. I really do know. IT WAS ONLY THE BLOODY CARLING CUP. The Mickey Mouse, none-of-the-big-boys-care Cup. Except, the thing was that in 2010-11 we did care. The manager did, ditching his kids-only policy for far stronger sides than he's selected in previous seasons. And so did the players, desperate to finally see some, dammit, *any* kind of pot-shaped reward for their efforts. None more so than Cesc Fabregas, who cruelly ended up missing the final with hamstring twang from a (as it eventually transpired, heartbreakingly irrelevant) league game against Stoke's travelling Orc army.

But perhaps most of all, it had come to mean something to the fans. Largely, what it meant was the chance to reset the miserable stopwatch that hangs around every pundit's neck, detailing down to the last nanosecond how long it's been since the Arsenal last won anything. At time of writing: 6 years, 3 months, 18 hours and 31 seconds. Ugh. All of us needed that monkey off our backs. In fact we needed that monkey off our backs and shot into space without so much as a Russian flag to wrap his tiny body in. "Fly, Dimitri, fly!" While I can't really excuse the hyperbole of saying that winning the Carling was my dream, I can at least try to explain it. You see as a relatively late Arsenal starter, I'd never seen one of our captains lifting a trophy in the flesh. And although technically we were still stuttering along in four competitions at the time, in the wake of the debacle at St James Park, and several other spectacular capitulations, the season was already starting to feel like quite the bum-clencher.

Having limped past such luminaries as Ipswich, Huddersfield and Leeds, I'd come to see the Carling not exactly as a sure thing, but certainly as sure as things ever got. By the time February 27th rolled around, I'd mentally built it up to be some unlikely combination of the Jules

Rimet trophy and getting my 500m swimming badge. It was to be the spark from which further glory would surely follow. No longer would our players resemble a small copse of haunted trees before big games. This. Was. It.

Or so we thought. The other half of 'we' being Arse2Mouse's co-blogger Dave Meikleham. At the time, both of us were working in Bath, writing about videogames for pennies, and had bonded over a mutually destructive love of the Arsenal. When the chance to rent a season ticket appeared on the company noticeboard we jumped on it, paying £500 each to split home fixtures stood at the back of the North Bank. On the eve of the season we began our blog, Arse2Mouse.com, partly because having thought up the name it seemed too good to waste, but also to provide a cathartic outlet for what we'd already taken to calling 'the madness'. Plus, every man needs a hobby, and blogging seems to be the 21st Century equivalent of fannying about in a shed.

If anything, though, Dave had built winning the Carling up to even more preposterous heights than I had. We were both exiles in the West Country, me from London, him from Edinburgh, but money matters had meant he'd decided to move back to Scotland before the end of the season. The final was to be his last match, and in our minds the glorious reward for months spent schlepping up and down to the Emirates. Little did I know at that point that his decision would mean seeing out the end of season Collapseo-rama© on my own, a sequence of games we now refer to simply as 'the death run'. Emotionally, though, we'd bet everything on seeing Robin – beautiful Robin, who wore the JVC shirt in his bedroom as a boy – lifting a trophy, now matter how clownish.

"We've got to get final tickets, ye auld fanny." This was how Dave invariably spoke to me. Every sentence finished with some flourish of Scotch invective. "Then, when Bowyer nets a last minute winner, we can noose ourselves fram the Wembley arch." But there was a problem. Thanks to Arsenal's Byzantine ticket allocation system, even though we'd racked up enough away games to qualify, they weren't assigned to our borrowed season ticket. And even if they had been, we'd only have been able to get one. Of course we considered burning our meagre savings on a tout. "Frig a dee, hen!" (Dave also favours insults that imply I'm a woman.) "Some lad on Twitter says he paid a scalper £680 for a pair. We cannae afford that." Hours were wasted on Google Chat, debating what we'd be willing to do to get tickets. Some of which involved unmentionable acts with tramps. "Wid ye let Harry Redknapp watch if it guaranteed we won?" I actually thought about that one. But as the game approached we'd all but resigned ourselves to going to a pub near the ground, when a call to a software contact finally came good. It's in the game, and so were we. Dave's reaction was as celebratory as I'd come to expect from him. "Nice work, neebur. We're definitely noosing ourselves now."

In the week before the match, whatever fragile confidence we had was washed out to sea by waves of self-inflicted doom. We were our own worst enemies; the low point being an hour spent pinging each other pictures via text of Birmingham players looking happy. Reading those conversations back now, we sound less like nervy fans and more like deranged cellmates. "I'll be awful company on the day, hen, ye ken that reet?" said Dave, over Google Chat. He even typed in Scottish. "Pure shaking with fear." And so we were. I think on some level, from almost as soon as I got out of bed on the big day, I knew something was going to go very badly wrong.

Part of the problem was that by this point we'd each come up with a bizarre suite of match-day superstitions. Some were fairly run of the mill: tapping wood after saying anything that might be jinxy about a player, wearing the same clothes to the game, that sort of thing. Others were weirder. When watching games on TV I'd taken to touching the ceiling whenever we were defending a set piece. I still don't know why, and clearly it wasn't very effective. Sandwiches had also become an issue after I'd cooked Dave a BLT at half-time during Braga away, which we went on to lose 2-0. "Nae more jinx sangers ye daftie!" On the morning of the final, my girlfriend, who remains astonishingly tolerant of this sort of bullshit, made us sausage sandwiches. Dave and I eyed them nervously; then dug in. With hindsight, that's probably when it all started to go south.

From that point on it's hard to remember a single thing going right. In their infinite idiocy, First Great Western had decided to put on a bus replacement service between Bath and Swindon in both directions. The same bus that habitually got us in at 2.00am on Champions League nights. "Imagine being on the bloody rattlebus back if we havenae won," muttered Dave, as we filed aboard alongside Gooners young and old. Arsenal were, of course, stick-on favourites, which brought with it its own voodoo kind of pressure. I scanned the other fans' faces for signs of confidence and didn't feel especially reassured by what I saw. We knew this: win and we wouldn't be given any credit. Lose and it'd be broken cannon logos in the papers again. I put my headphones on, hit play on the Arsecast, and wondered whether Gazidis and co had missed a trick in not selling club-branded brown paper bags to breathe into.

By the time we arrived in London it was pissing down. This was immediately identified as another dark omen. "Ye ken our team of dancing peacocks disnae perform well in the rain, fannybaws." Fraying nerves meant that the mood between Dave and I was unusually tense. We'd already almost fallen out over whether to wear colours – too jinxy, obviously – settling instead on scarves, and whether it was acceptable to place an insurance bet on Birmingham winning. (Him: pro. Me: violently anti.) The air of joylessness was enhanced by my refusal to drink pre-match, on the basis that I just wanted to get to the ground and get on with it, partly because I was worried our tickets weren't Kosher. They'd arrived as email attachments to be printed out, meaning we were walking up to (what felt like) the biggest game of our lives clutching two sheets of A4 with 'This is your ticket' written on them. "We're never getting in with these fanny tickets, barrygadge."

Before heading to Wembley we first met up with a half-Brazilian Gooner mate of mine from university, whose relentless positivity – "It'll be fine! It's only Birmingham! They're awful!" – only made us more panicky. Next we stopped to listlessly eat burgers and say hi to TheSquidboyLike, a fellow worrier I'd become friends with through Twitter, but never actually met previously. "This is no time for a man-date, ye fanny." Secretly, both Dave and I wished we could be with the old boys we'd got to know from the North Bank. Big Chris, Bald Steve and Toothless Dave. They'd all made us incredibly welcome over the course of the season, with their bleak humour and seen-it-all attitude. I felt less inclined to shit the bed with them around, but at that point they were somewhere in a proper boozer with tickets that had holograms on.

But it wasn't until we actually reached the stadium that the sense of impending doom really kicked in. Following the instructions on the tickets, we found ourselves funnelled up Wembley Way and into a sea of blue shirts. "This disnae feel reet," whispered Dave. But it was reet. We made our way to the Club Wembley entrance, flashed the homebrew tickets, and to our amazement were ushered inside into Wembley's yawning, soulless cavern of seemingly unfinished corridors and stairwells. I sat down to watch the remainder of West Ham unbuttoning Liverpool while Dave wandered off to buy two lagers that were as weak as they were expensive.

By the time he made it back I'd seen the team sheet and immediately relayed the bad news. "Whit?!" asked Dave, incredulous. "Knack's starting?!" That was our name for Tomas Rosicky, on account of his perma-banjaxed hamstrings. Nonetheless, even his presence hadn't entirely eradicated the flicker of hope we had. The likes of RVP, The Russian and Nasri were also starting, as was 'saucy' Jack. Surely we'd have enough. And so we made our way out of the guts of the stadium and into the light.

"Oh my god," hissed Dave.

"I know," I replied, scanning the blue and white all around us.

"But we're..."

"I fucking know, let's just get to the seats."

And so we stepped over seemingly endless Brummie legs, nodding and smiling sadly as we went, until we sat down with the enemy on either side. As far as I can tell Club Wembley is unsegregated due to the unlikelihood of anything worse than a few prawn sandwiches being thrown. But although there was the isolated pocket of Arsenal support, our side of Club Level was almost entirely blue-nosed. And the tiers above and below us were, of course, rammed with them. Some stripped to the waist, others bouncing beachballs; all making a right old racket. If we still had any doubts, they were gone now: this was going to be excruciating.

"I cannae dae it," whined Dave. "Think whit it'll be like if they score."

I sat there, eyes fixed forward, silently watching Arsenal's players warm up in a manner that couldn't have said 'casual' more without smooth jazz being played on Pat Rice's phone. As it was, we only had to wait 28 minutes to see exactly what a Birmingham goal was like. Always the entertainers, Arsenal had decided to run through a repertoire of the most hilarious moments from their travelling comedy revue. From a corner the ball was headed back into the box where Zigic – who's more a mobile gallows than an actual footballer – nodded the ball easily over Wojciech Szceszny. Zigic. We'd always said it would be him. Our half of the stadium erupted. Dave looked at me in the way I imagine cows do when they finally realise what they've been queuing for. "Plenty of time," I said, trying to sound reassuring as my stomach dissolved whatever was left of lunch instantly.

"Whit the fuck is wrong with Brum?" asked Dave, a few minutes later. "Why are they trying so hard?" And they were. Playing better than I can ever remember them doing before or after. Working hard all over the pitch, attacking with pace on the wings, limited players raising their game and fighting for each other. Every now and then Brum fans would turn to glance at us and smile. "They've been in turbo shat form and now they play like this. It's a pisstake."

Meanwhile, Arsenal shuffled and probed in the way we've come to know and not entirely love. Despite Birmingham's efforts, we we're still the better side, and the breakthrough came just before half-time – a neat, flowing move saw Wilshere crash a shot against the bar. The Russian collected the rebound, jinked his way to the byline and cut a chipped ball back to Robin Van Persie who hammered the volley in. We we're out of our seats bouncing, hugging. "RAAAAAAAAAAAAB!" shouted Dave. "GET IN!" But when we finally looked back at the pitch we realised another quintessentially Arsenalish moment was occurring. The skipper had hurt himself while scoring.

Half time arrived and we didn't move. I tried to check Twitter for news of the injury but couldn't get a signal. When RVP returned it was soon clear he wasn't quite right. The rest of the game passed in a blur, and although Birmingham seemed to be tiring, as the clock ticked down the realisation grew that one goal for either side would be enough. It came, inevitably, with a minute to go. Djourou missed his header, Koscielny shanked a clearance that should've been Szceszny's to scoop up, and Obafemi Martins, 46-years young, slotted home unchallenged. Cue somersaults on the pitch and bedlam all around us in the stands. It was the apotheosis, the crowning glory, of Arsenalish fuck-ups. Dave was immediately on his feet. "I'm off." I blocked his path with my leg. "Sit the fuck back down. There's still injury time." For a microsecond he cocked his fist back. I looked at him astonished. "You can leave if you want," I said quietly. "I'm seeing it out."

In Dave's defence I should point out this isn't the first time we've almost come to blows. When Sagna scored against Leeds I grabbed him so robustly that I jammed my thumb in his eye, slightly blacking it. In any case he relented and went back to his seat. For what that was worth. In the remaining minutes Martins almost scored again as we we're caught pressing for an equaliser. The final whistle blew and the Arsenal fans scattered in classic fire drill style. Outside, something strange happened. Obviously we weren't happy, but neither was the despair quite as deep as expected. In amongst the pain there was a sliver of relief. We lost. It was undoubtedly an embarrassing shambles. And we knew we'd be hearing about it for a while to come. But at least it was over.

"I definitely felt worse after Spurs," I said, trying to seem chirpy.

"Which one?" replies Dave.

"The 3-2 this year. That was awful. We were 2-0 up and I had to walk right past their fans at the end. Singing. Jesus. That was way worse."

"Nah, the 4-4 with them in '08 was the worst. We were two up with two minutes to go! I threw my program onto the pitch and got so drunk on the train I ended up in Cardiff."

And so it went all the way back to Bath, on the bloody rattlebus from bastard Wembley, swapping calamitous stories, and laughing about how it was only the Carling Cup anyway. The Mickey Mouse, none-of-the-big-boys-care Cup. Plus, we still had the Premier League, FA Cup and, whisper it, even the Champions League to go for. We'd already beaten Barcelona once for Bergkamp's sake!

Everything was going to be just fine.

Tim Clark is a professional videogames writer, part-time panicker and founder of Arse2Mouse.com, which is usually written on train journeys back to Bath from his seat in the North lower. Careful when you type the URL.

16

BEHIND THE 8-BALL

TIM BARKWILL

Back when football was still football, before the world came to watch, before we started to consume every single match from here, and then – because enough is never enough – every match from there, there was a time characterized by dwindling crowds, crumbling stadia, the threat of crowd violence and shorts that were so ridiculously short you wonder now how any of those gallant souls ever had children. The good old days? No: not even remotely.

For God's sake, Graham Taylor was lauded as a genius. And for our Club, for the great, the mighty Gunners, A to the F to the C, we, oh we were… well, our glory days came and went in the 1930's. We still remembered them. Not literally for most of us, but our dads remembered.

Back in the '30's, Arsenal were England. The unprecedented success brought to us by Herbert Chapman's five

league titles in a decade (two of which came to the team
Chapman had built after pneumonia had taken him from
us) guaranteed our place among the pantheon of footballing greats. This is not to say that success entirely eluded
AFC after the Chapman years. We won something in the
1940's, in the '50's and again in the '60's. We were the mas-
ters of the intermittent blip on the radar.

Then, out of the blue, we did the Double in the 1970's
(probably just to proffer a slap in the face to our local rivals
who'd done the same thing in the decade prior), before
embarking on our magnificent FA Cup final three-peat
('78-'80). Quite an achievement, even if glory managed
to elude us on all but one of those occasions. The years
following were lean. Did the disappointment of Trevor
Brooking's header psychologically scar us? Perhaps: but
probably not as deeply as Willie Young's studs scarred Paul
Allen.

No; the truth of it was Brady left for the continent, Rixy
never quite lived up to his promise, Stapleton moved on
and since Clive Allen looked too much like a goal scorer we
immediately swapped him for a left-back. Admittedly the
left-back we picked up proved to be the best in the country, but he wasn't about to enliven the "goals for" column.
Of course, our history had never been remarkable for
achievements in that column. Yet we remained consistently
threatening, always likely to prove a contender thanks to
our parsimony rather than any flair. The mirror opposite of

our neighbours, the enemy in white and blue which is, of course, where Allen ended up, possibly seeking revenge for young Willie's timeless scything down of his cousin. And it was galling to have to have to sit back and watch that lot from the wrong end of the Seven Sisters road trundle off to F.A. Cup glory with Chas 'n' Dave two years in a row while we worked hard to achieve mid-table mediocrity.

During the early-80's (Terry Neill's last years in charge) we were often so poor that mid-table seemed like a grand stroke of good fortune. At the time, however, we always *believed* that we could achieve success, but we believed in that Arsenal way; not as though you actually thought it likely to transpire, more that the law of averages had to kick in at some point. We believed in the team in that way you believe when rolling your eyes towards heaven while not really believing at all. But we kept turning up. Kept buying the programmes. Kept piling up the discarded peanut shells around our feet. Come rain or … well, more rain.

In 1983 Terry Neill departed and Don Howe took over. Unfortunately Howe fared little better and in 1986 he was replaced by George Graham. With the introduction of Graham as manager the fortunes of AFC changed quite radically. We cultivated a certain style and even came close to topping the goal-scoring charts. From that point on the history of Arsenal became ever more entwined with success, culminating in the appointment of Wenger and the move away from Highbury to Ashburton Grove.

But our focus here is not on success. We're not going to eulogise the game with which we've become all too familiar over the last decade or so. Rather, we're looking back into those dark days – and they literally do seem wintry and dark – of the old First Division; one that existed before the dazzle of the Premiership, before the money. When the most foreign player on your team would be a lad from Dublin.

Why, for God's sake, would you want to cast us back into those dull doldrums of despond? Please tell us this isn't going to turn into one of those "You don't know when you're well off" lectures, rattling on like one of the four horsemen of Yorkshire:

"A round ball?! We was lucky to have a lump of coal to kick around in our bare feet with nails in our toes on a lava flow with our own severed arms stood for goalposts! Aye, lad."

Fine. I'll not browbeat in an effort to brighten the outlook by contrast. If only because, in truth, I didn't think those dull, dark days were so bad. I mean, yes, of course they were bad, but they taught us a lot. It's one thing to walk into the arms of a club riding the crest of a wave called success, it's quite another to fall in love with one whose fortunes are waning. Yet this was how I first came to know and love the Gunners.

In matters of the heart, there are no rules; rhyme and reason disappear from view. You just fall. Sometimes you get hurt. But if you're a romantic type then it doesn't matter how many times you get hurt or how badly, you can't help but love. Today, we'd call that a dysfunctional relationship. The only thing keeping us sane is the knowledge that we're not alone. There are others out there, just like us. Proudly holding high our masochistic streaks as though banners of allegiance. Shouldn't there be some sort of support group?

The last time I saw the red and white take the field was at Highbury, from the West Stand Upper. The same location, give or take a few rows, that my Dad and I occupied for years. Even though we held no season tickets, in those days the supply exceeded the demand and getting a seat wasn't hard at all. In front of us were a gaggle of lads, born and bred in North London, Arsenal through and through. They always had handfuls of peanuts, somehow managing to eat them in-between joyously shouting at the events unfolding before us. They were vocal, continually smiling and joking (usually at the expense of our own players), articulate in that way Londoners can be if you can keep up with the 100 mph delivery. I was a child who took himself and his team too seriously. I rarely saw the funny side of anything to do with the football we played. There was too much at stake. Every game was life or death. At least, that's how it felt (which is, perhaps, why I failed to see the funny side of Paul Davis).

Paul was a young lad when he broke into the first team. In those days your starting eleven almost never changed. Injury? What injury? Well, obviously he's missing a foot, but it's his left one he plays with so no problem. When a player got into the first team that player stayed in the first team. Paul arrived, a London boy, born and bred. He made his debut away to the enemy, down White Heart's Shame; a 2-1 victory on April 7th, 1980. We didn't go to away matches in those days. The threat of hooliganism hung over matches. Though exaggerated by the sensationalism of the tabloids from the 70's onward, it was still real enough.

Anyway, I didn't see Paul until he stepped out on the hallowed soil of our pristine patch. Do I remember the game? No; but then most games blend together a bit at that time. A goal-less draw here, a score draw there, a scrappy one-nil to keep the mystery alive. What I do remember most of all, is Davis himself. A thin bloke who looked like strong gust would take him away. And by God was he awful. I mean terribly, ludicrously bad. Couldn't make a pass. Tackling was atrocious. Walking in a straight line seemed to be about all he could manage without somehow making the kind of mistake that gives every player nightmares.

Still, I loved that team. I loved each player on that team. It used to hurt me when the gaggle would mock some of them. They were my players. Why couldn't everyone love them as I did? But then Paul showed up and everything changed. He was the first player I ever heard booed when his name was read out on the team sheet before kick off. It wasn't the kind of cruel, heartless booing you get sometimes at public events. No, it was more the booing of the pantomime villain. As if everyone knew how bad he was going to be each time he played and the audience took a perverse delight in letting him know they knew. Was it peer pressure that made me join in? There was only my Dad alongside me, so that can't be it. So what then? Desire to mix with the tribe? A latent wish to be as one with the cool gaggle who came from here, lived their lives on the doorstep while I, just a tourist, lived in Kent?

No. It was all a part of growing up, that part of growing up where you learn not to take things so seriously. When you learn that it's okay to laugh at your heroes. In fact, it's good to do so because the world won't often bow to your will and you discover you can't wish things into being. No matter how hard you try, you can't control the errant passing of a Paul Davis, our number 8.

Now, if that had been it, if that was the be all and end all of my relationship with Paul Davis, it'd still be significant enough to have left an indelible imprint upon me. He'd have been the 'hero' I came to laugh at. He would have helped me learn that it's okay to laugh at the game and the players. But that's not why I remember Paul Davis. That's not even *how* I remember Paul Davis. What I remember is a player whose skill and style were the closest thing to Jean Tigana I've ever seen in English football. What I remember is a player whose touch and passing outshone any other player on the field. A man who tackled like his shoulders were twice as broad as they were and he packed

20 extra kilos of pure muscle cunningly disguised by his waifish frame. What I remember is a player who consistently showed up and brought his best game.

I know! You're thinking this Paul Davis and the Paul Davis who couldn't put a foot right have to be two different people. If only they were – it would have made my life so much simpler. Alas, life is never simple. And so it was that the lesson Paul Davis really taught me was far more valuable. The pariah we all booed, while having a good chuckle, turned out to be the true story of the ugly duckling, who in the season following, blossomed into the most elegant swan I ever saw in the red and white. How? What? Huh?

I wish there were some logical explanation for it. Some simple formula we could refer back to and say, 'Ahhh… that's how it happened,' but, of course, there isn't. Paul Davis went from being a liability to the cornerstone of our salvation, and the only reason was time. There wasn't any miracle. Paul had always been a superbly gifted footballer, but when you're young it's difficult to get up to speed and your game gets thrown. The crowd is merciless. They used to watch Christians vs. Lions. So it was, the transformation of Paul Davis taught me to never trust to first impressions. What you see is *not* always what you get. It pays to be patient, to keep your counsel, rather than pass judgment before the jury has been given adequate time to reach their verdict. Can you imagine that today's game? It's just not possible, is it?

The MTV-generation gave us the 30-second attention span and Queen supplied the anthem, letting us know precisely what we wanted and when we wanted it. Patience has become an archaic concept that'll be soon routed from the dictionaries of Western civilization. It's no-one's fault. We all contribute. We know too much. We believe we've seen it all before. The punchline told mid-joke. Yet Paul Davis proved that if you invest a little time and have a little faith, great talent can grow and flourish from seemingly barren ground.

Because I had the privilege of watching the transformation of Paul Davis, I never gave up on Alex Song. Despite the woeful performances in his first matches for us, I recalled the ugly duckling and trusted in the coaching staff, who all predicted great things for Alex. He's no Paul Davis, mind, but, really, how many of those come along in a lifetime? And that's the funny thing; few remember Paul Davis for his skill. Perhaps we were all still too downhearted by the departure of Brady and the disappointment in Rix to look closely enough to see that in Paul Davis we had found our 'cultured left foot' in the middle of the park. He wasn't a goal scorer like Brady, that kind of classic number 10 the continentals would call the playmaker, the guy who makes everything tick in attack. But in his subtle way, Paul was the fulcrum. In the absence of a playmaker, he made the plays with his astute passing, his range, his tackling; his ability to read the game and make interceptions before running at the opposition's penalty area. We'd always thought of the playmaker living in the final third, but Paul Davis showed that he can lie deep and dictate play from all over the field. He was everything a midfielder should be: our number eight: the ugly duckling.

Yet, even the moral of the ugly duckling story is not the greatest lesson Paul Davis taught me. More important than any of the valuable lessons I've already mentioned is this: Paul Davis taught me what it means to persevere. Right from the first, he always tried to get involved. He'd never try to hide on the pitch or shy away. Just ask Glenn Cockerill.

It happened at the Dell, a game against Southampton back in '88. Cockerill was a mouthy git with a terrible haircut (even for the '80's it was bad). During a match Cockerill took it upon himself to verbally abuse Davis. Davis took it upon himself to wait for a lull in the game and then clock Cockerill, breaking his jaw. Paul Davis, the waif, *broke* the jaw of Glenn Cockerill, the 6' 3', self-styled all-action 'hard man' midfielder. No-one would've believed it if the T.V. cameras hadn't picked it up – leading to a ret-rospective nine-match ban for our number 8!

My Dad didn't believe it. When he first heard what hap-pened, he laughed and asked if I was sure Davis hadn't broken himself rather than someone else. Not that Paul Davis could ever be considered a lightweight. He grafted in every match, but he wasn't a dirty player. Certainly he was not the kind to commit professional fouls and not the kind to resort to physical violence (although, if memory serves, he was there at Old Trafford in October '90, and he certainly didn't shy away from confrontation on that occasion).

I left England before Paul Davis left Arsenal. The Arsenal I've watched since has played with style and power, then style and grace, achieving or not achieving along the way. Trophies have been collected; more are expected. It's a far cry from the game I knew, but I still follow the team religiously. It's not the same as being there at the ground – at that magnificent new home, that I've yet to see first-hand – but I watch every game courtesy of television or the 'Net. Keeping an eye out for the next Paul Davis: the next Arsenal legend.

A failed director turned failed screenwriter, T.J. Barkwill's life is most remarkable for the ten years he spent incarcerated in an Alsatian jail before his warders realized he wasn't a dog and set him free. His favourite player isn't, rather it's an entire midfield and it played for France in 1986.

17

ON ARSENAL'S FINANCES – A GAME OF TWO HALVES

KIERON O'CONNOR

Many years ago, I used to stand on the North Bank watching the likes of Liam Brady, Frank Stapleton and David O'Leary doing their stuff for Arsenal. From my regular vantage point on the terraces, my only thoughts were whether we would win, though I did allow myself to marvel at Alan Sunderland's haircut and wonder why Willie Young always wore a shirt a size too small for him. Although that side never really challenged in the league, it did get to the FA Cup final three years in a row, allowing me to treat a trip to Wembley as an annual event. Twice we lost, though those defeats seem like a product of my imagination. Honestly, how could we concede goals to Roger Osborne (who?) and a header from Trevor Brooking? Even the 3-2 triumph against Manchester United left me an emotional wreck, as we threw a way a two-goal lead, only to score the winner in injury time.

In 1980 I remember bunking off school to make my way up from Brighton to Highbury for the Cup Winners' Cup semi-final against Juventus, and thinking that we had blown it when we could only draw 1-1. How wrong I was. Two weeks later, I was listening on my transistor radio as Paul Vaessen's last minute header took us through. Cue pandemonium in my bedroom. Of course, we then lost the final to Valencia on penalties, and my mother heard for the first time the full range of my profanities. In short, I fully identified with this team and am not ashamed to admit that I shed a few tears when Juventus got their revenge by taking "Chippy" off our hands.

Not for a single moment did I worry about the club's balance sheet or think that the club's shirt would look better emblazoned with the name of a sponsor. However, times have changed. I now earn my corn in the world of finance and people seem just as interested in matters off the pitch these days. Even if Arsenal slump to a defeat, we can console ourselves with the knowledge that at least our bottom line looks good.

Well, that's sort of true, but Arsenal's finances are more like the proverbial "game of two halves." There's plenty of good stuff there, but also a few weaknesses which have affected our ability to compete at the very highest levels. That said, there's no doubt that our financials have been far better than most. Take the last annual results from 2009/10, which were quite superb – with revenue of £380 million and profit before tax of £56 million both setting new record highs for the club. As chief executive Ivan Gazidis observed, with commendable understatement, these results were "very healthy".

In truth, that's a seriously impressive performance, especially if you consider that only three other Premier League clubs made profits in 2010 and all of those were significantly smaller than ours. To place this into context, the three teams that finished ahead of us last season all recorded massive losses: Manchester United £80 million, Chelsea £70 million and Manchester City, making the others look like amateurs, an incredible £121 million. It is a rare thing indeed for football clubs to make money, but Arsenal have managed to do this for many years. The last time that we reported a loss was eight years ago, way back in 2002, while total profits have been rising ever since the move to the Emirates stadium: 2007 £6 million, 2008 £37 million, 2009 £46 million and 2010 £56 million. In the last three years alone, Arsenal have produced combined pre-tax profits of £138 million – an astonishing figure in the world of football, which is more accustomed to turning billionaires into millionaires.

That's certainly not the case for our club. Excluding income from property development, Arsenal's revenue has nearly doubled in the last five years from £115 million to £223 million, which is second only to Manchester United among English clubs (£286 million) and places us fifth in Deloitte's Money League.

However, as the legendary investor Warren Buffett advised, "a rising tide floats all boats", so it might just be that all football clubs have experienced similar revenue growth. In other words, our revenue growth might not be down to our board's genius, but due to the extra money pouring into football. "Up to a point, Lord Copper", as Evelyn Waugh once memorably wrote, given that the big four clubs in England have all significantly increased their revenue in this period. Then again, the figures do show that we have outperformed our peers. We have overtaken Chelsea's revenue, even during a period of sustained success for West London's nouveaux riches; widened the difference with Liverpool, and slightly closed the gap with Manchester United.

Where money has been growing for football clubs everywhere is, of course, television. Many fans could do without the weekly inanities of the Sky pundits, but, in fairness, "he who pays the piper, calls the tune" and there is no doubt that Murdoch's men pay a pretty penny for their TV rights with Arsenal receiving a distribution from the Premier League of well over £50 million a season. Interestingly, this is where Gooners abroad indirectly help the club's finances, as it is the overseas rights that are driving the hefty increases in TV money.

Arsenal are also part of the select group that have benefited from the Champions League, receiving £27 million from UEFA for each of the last two years. Even though the club's progress in Europe's flagship tournament has been getting worse over the last three seasons, the revenue has been improving, mainly thanks to a new cycle of broadcasting contracts. Gazidis has claimed that Arsenal budget so that the club could survive missing a year of Champions league football without selling players, but these figures once again demonstrate the importance of qualification to Europe's elite.

Unlike the vast majority of other clubs, the principal reason for our revenue growth is not television, but match day income. Since the club moved to the new stadium, this revenue stream has more than doubled from £44 million to £94 million, which has had a massive impact on total turnover and justifies the board's courageous decision to leave Highbury, at least from a financial perspective, even though I for one miss the North Bank terribly. With a capacity of just over 60,000, the Emirates can accommodate 22,000 more fans than that famous old ground, generating an additional £50 million revenue per season. Clearly the costs of running a bigger operation are higher, but it's still positive financially with each home game generating revenue of around £3.5 million. That is a striking figure, especially when you consider that Manchester United earn only slightly more per match, even though the capacity at Old Trafford is much higher at 76,000.

In fact, our match day revenue is the third highest in Europe with most matches selling out and the club advise us that there is a 40,000 waiting list for season tickets. That's all very well, but I'm not sure that it justifies the misguided decision to increase ticket prices by 6.5% this season. Although part of this is down to the 2.5% VAT rise, the remaining inflationary increase is a bitter pill to swallow for fans that already pay among the highest prices in world football. In the business world, price increases are often considered the path of least resistance, and football club owners are proving increasingly happy to adopt the same approach, as their "customers" have the fiercest brand loyalty around. After all, you and I are hardly likely to switch our allegiance to Spurs. So, we are a cash-generating machine, but that does not mean that we have a perfect business model. Oh no.

If you take a closer look under the bonnet, there are some underlying issues that suggest that the financial picture is not quite so wonderful as it has been painted. In fact, if the £11 million property profit and the £38 million made from player sales were excluded, the remaining football profit in 2010 would have only been £7 million. That's still very respectable compared to most clubs, but highlights the importance of these two exceptional factors to Arsenal's results. There is little doubt that the club has benefited from property development, though the profit of £11 million is not quite as high as you might expect given the £157 million revenue from this activity. Don't get me wrong, that profit is still better than a kick in the face, but it's a lot smaller than the £45 million football profit. In other words, it's still football that's driving the business (though sometimes it may feel like the other way round).

Although the club almost certainly anticipated higher profits when the Highbury Square developments was launched, the gains actually represent a good turnaround from a couple of years ago, when the slump in the property market forced the club to extend the repayment deadline on the bank loan to reflect delays in sales completion. That said, we can now anticipate some hefty windfall gains from property sales in terms of surplus cash, so the calculated gamble on the property development strategy has just about paid off. Nevertheless, Gazidis pointed out that the club could not afford to be over-reliant on bricks and mortar, "The profits from property are temporary and we need to make sure that in the longer term costs remain at a level which can be paid from our football revenues."

Those football revenues have been inflated in previous years by excess gains on player sales. In 2010 this was beautifully explained by our old-school chairman Peter Hill-Wood, "profits were boosted by some £38 million from the sales of players who were no longer central to Wenger's future plans", in an acidic reference to the transfer of Emmanuel Adebayor and Kolo Touré to the ever-generous Manchester City. This is nothing new, as we have averaged £25 million profit on player sales every season since the move to the Emirates, making good money from stars who were past their sell-by date (Vieira, Henry, Touré) or were disruptive influences in the dressing room (Cole, Adebayor). The lack of big money sales last season, with only Eduardo's move to Shakhtar Donetsk earning reasonable money, will therefore have a major impact on our financials for 2011, where the football business is likely to be around the break-even level, instead of the large profits of previous years. Of course, this will again change in 2012 after a summer of major sales (Fabregas, Nasri, Clichy and Eboue). However, it is questionable whether it is the right strategy to continually sell our best players. Whereas we have held the upper hand in such transactions in years gone by, the departures of Fabregas and Nasri somehow felt different. To be blunt, my concern is that this might lead to a similar decline to the one we experienced after Brady's departure in the 80s.

The area that has really restricted our ability to operate at the higher end of the transfer market is the woeful commercial income of £44 million, which lags way behind the rest of Europe's leading clubs, e.g. Bayern Munich £142 million and Real Madrid £123 million generate three times as much revenue here, while Manchester United have just broken the £100 million barrier. The weakness arises from the fact we had to tie ourselves into long-term deals to provide security for the stadium financing, which arguably made sense at the time, but recent deals by other clubs have highlighted the lost opportunities. The Emirates deal was worth £90 million, covering 15 years of stadium naming rights (£42 million) running until 2021 and eight years of shirt sponsorship (£48 million) until 2014. Similarly, we signed a seven-year kit supplier deal with Nike for £55 million, but that has since been extended by three years until 2013/14. Following step-ups, the shirt sponsorship deal is reportedly worth £5.5 million a season, which compares very unfavourably to the £20 million earned by Liverpool from Standard Chartered and Manchester United from Aon. It's the same story with the kit deal, which now delivers £8 million a season, compared to the £25 million deals enjoyed by Liverpool with Warrior Sports and Manchester United with Nike (yes, the same company that pays Arsenal much less). It's not overly dramatic to say that we leave £30-40 million a season on the table, because of these poor commercial deals, which would fund the purchase of one great player.

Little wonder that the club said, "There is no doubt that the areas of commercial activity and sponsorship provide the greatest opportunity for the Group to generate significant incremental revenues in the medium to long term." That's one way of putting it. Although some encouraging deals have been signed with secondary sponsors recently, the bar is continually being raised, as seen by Manchester City's amazing deal with Etihad and Manchester United securing £10 million a season from DHL for their training kit. It really is about time that Arsenal's much-vaunted (well, certainly expensive) commercial team pulled their collective finger out.

More revenue is certainly required, in order that we can afford a wage bill that allows us to compete with other leading clubs. There's certainly been explosive growth in wages, which have risen from £83 million to £111 million in just four years and will again "show a significant increase" in 2011, but this is not really enough these days. In fact, our wage bill is still substantially less than Chelsea (£173 million), Manchester City (£133 million) and Manchester United (£132 million) and just behind Liverpool (£114 million). On the other hand, it is also a lot higher than the chasing pack. In particular, it is a hefty £44 million more than Tottenham (£67 million), who finished just one place lower in the Premier League.

This sometimes comes as a surprise to many fans, given the well-publicised self-sufficient model, but is due to a couple of factors. We have a large squad and, while the wages at the top end might not be the highest, fringe players like Denilson and Diaby are handsomely awarded, as are the young players. In addition, we frequently re-sign players on long-term contracts, which represents "the best means of protecting the value of one of our most important assets", at least according to Hill-Wood. This is a policy that is well worth reviewing, as it might be more productive to allocate more of the wage bill to the first team.

The price we paid to move into a spanking new stadium was to take on a lot of debt. We have managed to pay off the substantial property development loans, but the club still has gross debt of £263 million, which effectively represents the long-term mortgage on the Emirates Stadium. That said, once cash balances of £128 million are deducted, net debt is down to only £136 million, which is a significant reduction from the £318 million peak in 2008. However, we are still paying around £20 million a year to service these loans. That may be considerably less than the huge interest payments suffered by Manchester United and Liverpool, but it's still a lot of cash to take away from the annual budget. Put another way, that would cover the wages of four quality players earning £100,000 a week.

It's not clear whether it would be possible to pay off the outstanding debt early in order to reduce the interest charges, but my guess is that the board is in no hurry to do so, as Gazidis has argued that not all debt is bad, "The debt that we're left with is what I would call 'healthy debt' – it's long term, low rates and very affordable for the club". That's all very well, but as transfer windows come and go with Arsenal seemingly reluctant to shop at the higher end of the transfer market, the fans have become increasingly puzzled about this strange state of affairs. Indeed, some sections of the crowd have taken to urging the club to spend some money, though this message is usually delivered with a great deal more bluntness.

The reality is that we have consistently spent less than our rivals over the last few years in the transfer market. In the era of foreign ownership, Arsenal are the only top club to actually make money from buying and selling players, while Chelsea and Manchester City have spent over £400 million each. Although reported transfer fees are notoriously unreliable, it is beyond dispute that other clubs' net spend is significantly higher with Liverpool, Manchester United and even Spurs all above £100 million in the same period. Arsène Wenger has steadfastly refused to endanger Arsenal's financial security by splashing out large sums on over-priced, big name players. For Arsenal to spend not just less, but so much less than these clubs and still challenge for honours is testament to the incredible job that the Frenchman has done with the funds available, but is it enough these days? The landscape of English football has changed dramatically in the last few years with the arrival of Roman Abramovich at Chelsea and Sheikh Mansour at Manchester City. Arsenal's "commitment to a financially self-sustaining business model" is admirable, but it is very difficult to maintain when you are competing against billionaires for whom money is no object.

A strong balance sheet might be praiseworthy, but it should not be the club's primary objective, as even Hill-Wood admitted, "Our business goal is not to generate profits as such, but rather to grow the club's revenues, so that they can be re-invested in the team and the long-term success of the club". This begs the obvious question as to why has Wenger been so reluctant to spend? There is no doubt that the move to the new stadium limited the transfer budget over the past few years, but the financial situation has greatly improved and it is clear that funds are available to buy the players that the team needs. However, there is still a suspicion that the manager would prefer to build rather than buy, so much of the low spending seems to be out of choice. Indeed, Gazidis clarified the club's stance last year, "We believe transfer spending is the last resort. That's a sensible view to have. Re-signing players is a far more efficient system".

Wenger is clearly singing from the same song sheet, as he has reiterated his preference for developing young players to dipping into the transfer market, "If I go out and buy players, then Jack Wilshere doesn't come through". He gave a further insight into his thoughts, when he argued, "The job of a manager is not to spend as much money as possible."

That was then, this is now.

This summer, it became abundantly clear that the side needed strengthening in order to add some experience and steel to the young talents already there, especially after the high-profile departures of Fabregas and Nasri, hence the "supermarket sweep" on transfer deadline day. There were even rumours about huge bids for the likes of Eden Hazard, Yann M'Vila and Mario Götze, so it looks like the strategy might be beginning to change. Arsenal had hoped that their prudent approach would be rewarded by the imminent arrival of UEFA's Financial Fair Play regulations, which aim to force clubs to live within their means. In theory, this should mean that the age of the big spender will be drawing to an end, which would benefit clubs like Arsenal who will have no problem complying with the new rules. However, although many clubs have cut back on their spending, the law of unintended consequences might also apply. Specifically, some clubs seem to have opted to improve profitability by increasing their revenue through a plethora of new sponsorship deals, rather than reducing transfers and wages. This may be only a temporary phenomenon, but it's no longer a slam-dunk that Arsenal's approach will flourish under FFP.

This might explain the seeming about-turn this transfer window, when Arsenal finally splashed the cash, though it might also be due to new owner Stan Kroenke exerting some influence, as he will surely want to be associated with a winning club. Even though he is one of the wealthiest men on the planet, he gives every sign of being a careful investor. Ideally, he would be in no hurry for major change, but the situation was becoming desperate after a very shaky start to the season, including the 8-2 humiliation at the hands of Manchester United. You have to believe that Kroenke encouraged Arsène into acting more decisively when pursuing new players.

One great opportunity for the American to make an immediate impact would be to pay off the club's debt early in order to reduce the annual interest costs and free up money saved for improving the squad. Frankly, given Kroenke's praise for Arsenal's self-sustaining model, this does not seem too likely, but other club owners have been known to go down this path. Another way of looking at our strategy is to ask whether we can afford not to spend, especially as others seem happy to buy their way to success. The traditional "Sky Four" has been gate crashed by the extremely wealthy Manchester City and the big-spending Tottenham, so Arsenal can no longer take it for granted that they will secure the lucrative Champions League qualification.

Not only did the collapse towards the end of last season prove disappointing to us fans, but it also hurt Arsenal's bank balance. The impact of dropping from second to fourth place meant that the Premier League merit payment was lower, but the damage did not stop there, as it also reduces the distribution from the following season's Champions League, which partly depends on that finishing position. In other words, a little more effort on the pitch would have brought higher financial rewards, which might just have avoided the need to raise ticket prices. Consider that for a moment.

Furthermore, it is evident that sponsors like to be associated with winners, so this should also be a consideration when it comes to deciding how much to spend on buying new players. That ignores the increase in shirt sales and other merchandising that normally results from a club having a world-class player or two on its books.

In summary, our finances are in a somewhat strange position at the moment. Yes, our commercial income is much lower than it should be for a club like ours, but we still enjoy the fifth highest revenue in Europe (excluding any money from property sales), so we are hardly standing in line for the poor house. What is needed, in my humble opinion, is a more sophisticated use of those resources. That means spending less on under-performing squad players to free up funds for those experienced, world class individuals that can make a significant difference. There were encouraging signs of this happening this summer, so fingers crossed that the lessons of the past few unsuccessful seasons have been taken on board. Then, in three years time, the cavalry should arrive in the form of thumping great new commercial deals.

Whatever happens, Arsenal will be my team through all the highs and lows. My hair is a lot greyer than those days when I stood on the North Bank as a teenager, but the emotions remain unchanged. Every defeat still hurts, every victory still puts a smile on my face for the rest of the weekend. There's little doubt that football has become big business, but when I think about Arsenal, my first thoughts are not for the balance sheet, but the glorious sporting moments, many of which I now have to enjoy through the wonders of cable television, as I've lived abroad for 25 years. Like the evening I spent in Milan watching Michael Thomas' "It's up for grabs now" moment, when I set the

Italian record for the highest jump from a sitting position; or the afternoon in Zürich when Tony Adams sealed the title with *that* goal.

In short, football finances are important, but let's not forget that it's just a means to an end and it's the football that makes it the beautiful game.

Kieron O'Connor writes The Swiss Ramble, a blog focusing on the business of football. He used to stand on the North Bank, but now watches Arsenal from Switzerland via the wonders of satellite TV.

18

SUPPORTING ARSENAL FROM AFAR

LEANNE HURLEY

When it comes to being a 'far-flung' Arsenal supporter I'm luckier than most in that I'm not actually that far flung. Living in Belfast means I am only a few hours via plane, train, and automobile from the Emirates (something many would give their left one, and that of someone close to them).

Growing up in Northern Ireland I was introduced to football by my grandfather at the age of four. The choice of football back then was Irish League, while English football wasn't anything more than Man United or Liverpool, with a televised match once a week. Easter and New Year were a veritable football fest when we might have been spoiled with two, maybe even three, matches.

I didn't know much about football then. I was quite possibly the only female who went to matches in Northern

Ireland, but I knew I didn't want to support either United or Liverpool. Some would point to my contrary nature but I prefer to believe that some are just born with sense. When it came to footballing matters I knew, even at a young age, those teams weren't the ones for me. So, with a father who was a rugby fan, a grandfather who had no interest outside the Irish League, and little or no football coverage beyond United and Liverpool, I got on with supporting a bunch of Irish league part-timers playing hoofball on a rectangle of mud.

It wasn't until 1987 (when I was 11), that Arsenal finally made their way into my heart; a place they would come to own, fill with joy and tear apart with no regard for my feelings or my life away from football. It was a school trip to Germany, a round trip of some 1800 miles by coach with an overnight stop in London on the way home. For some reason the school booked a trip around Highbury and from the moment the coach pulled up outside that magnificent stadium on Avenell Road I was hooked.

It has only been in recent years I have been able to afford to go and see Arsenal play; usually against the Blackburns and Sunderlands of this world as they are the matches it is easier to get tickets for. In these financially tough times, I don't get to as many matches as I used to or would like. I never got to see Arsenal play at Highbury, yet the stadium feels as important to me as it does to any other Gooner. I was lucky enough to have had one opportunity to walk on (well, near) the hallowed turf at the Highbury, as well as see some of the players on the pitch as they posed for photographs with the Littlewoods Cup. If I'd had a bit more of a clue back then I'd have paid more attention, but as it was, I was just so blown away by the surroundings and Highbury itself that I paid only a fleeting glance to the players (I think it was David O'Leary and someone else).

Following Arsenal while not being able to get to games regularly has not been easy, but I know I'm fortunate in that I've actually been able to see the love of my life in the flesh. Many others aren't so lucky and I know this it is a bone of contention with some fans, who believe you should truly only support your local team. That's a view I simply do not ascribe to, not because I don't live near Arsenal, but because if not for the international fans we would be a much poorer club. And I don't just mean financially.

Supporting from afar is not always easy; there can be a sense of isolation –somewhat helped by the arrival of social media sites such as Twitter. Whereas before the only real choices were to watch at home with as many friends as you could squeeze into your house (if you were fortunate enough to have friends who wanted to watch Arsenal), or head to your local pub (not always practical due to location or religious beliefs), now you can watch with thousands of other 'virtual' Gooners online. While it might not give the same buzz as being surrounded by a sixty thousand actual

Arsenal fans, it has fostered a sense of community and offered a space to show that we are not alone in our footballing madness. Now, you can have instant reaction from fans around the world, you can view and respond to the opinions of others, engage in debate; and while Twitter will never replace the feeling of actually being at the Emirates, it does afford Gooners the chance to share their joy, pain and disbelief at what they are watching in a way that few ever imagined.

If the worst thing about being a far flung Gooner is not being able to get to games, or see their heroes in the flesh, the best thing is feeling part of the global Gooner community, something quite impossible pre-Internet. There are plenty of other benefits too, such as fewer Spurs fans, not having to read The Sun, and it never being too warm at 4am to wear an Arsenal scarf. A common complaint heard by far flung supporters is abuse for not being 'real' fans as they don't live in N5, but thankfully that tends to come from a vocal minority and is not reflective of how most Gooners who live near Arsenal feel. Should we really let something as arbitrary as where a person was born, or where they live, dictate who is a real fan and who is not?

Sometimes arguments ensue between those who go every week and those who can't, and valid points are raised, all the while missing the obvious. It isn't the amount you spend that makes you a 'proper' fan; it's the amount it takes out of you.

We all want the same for Arsenal, that is, success on the pitch. How the club go about achieving that will always divide fans. Some want to spend, some want to promote from within, some want to trust that the manager might know better than the rest of us. Some want to see pretty football, some want to win at all costs. Others think that if only we'd signed player X from club Y we would be doing better, while others believe if we hadn't signed player A from club B we'd be doing even better. It's complicated, like life, but it is just football.

There are many around the world who will never get to experience being at an Arsenal game first-hand, yet these people still support the club, our club, their club, because that's what supporters do. We shouldn't care about distances or regular attendance; we should care about the quality of support. We have some of the greatest fans in the world, spread right across the globe, and we are lucky to have them. The dedication of Arsenal fans across the globe is really something all Arsenal fans should be proud of. There isn't a time zone we don't occupy, a continent we don't claim as our own, or a time considered too ridiculous to get up and watch The Arsenal.

Living far from the Emirates does not exclude you from being a fan and as Arsenal's tour of the Far East in the summer of 2011 proved, some of our most passionate fans live far and wide. Witness the Chinese fans with their magnificent banner: *Barce pay £40m take Cesc away or go home to wank* [sic]. They take every crumb that falls their way and they are grateful for it. Football is now a global industry with all clubs making more and more of an effort to include those fans who do not live on their doorsteps. We all hold close our memories of our favourite Arsenal goal; the player we longed to see in the flesh but never got the opportunity; the matches we wished we could have been there for; for those fortunate to witness them in person the memory might be different, but the events are the same for those watching from afar. We remember where we were when Henry blasted past Barthez, or when Bergkamp spun the Newcastle defence, to score what is regarded as Arsenal's best goal of all time. We wear our shirts with pride and we defend our club as if it was a member of our own family because, well, it is.

Arsenal are in all of our hearts no matter how we came to start supporting the team. We feel the pain and humiliation of a bad defeat just as deeply as those who were there, perhaps even more so, because we know that we missed the chance to be there to cheer the players on. In troubled times such as this, the demon year of 2011, we feel further from our club because we feel helpless. We want to be there, to lift the spirits, to support: isn't that what 'supporters' do?

We know that the players and the managers won't read our words on the internet or hear our anguished cries which echo around our living rooms, but we still get up at 4 and 5am no matter what time we start work. We still stay up until late, if only for the chance of watching Arsenal from hundreds and thousands of miles away.

We are still Gooners, no matter our postcode, and together, we make up the largest and most united Global footballing community on the planet and that is something we should all be extremely proud of.

Leanne Hurley runs LadyArse.com. She has been an Arsenal fan since 1987, a blogger since 2008, and a mouthpiece since birth.

19

STRENGTH FROM WITHIN: FROM MEE TO GRAHAM

DAVID FABER

I suppose if I were to suggest to supporters born in the late 40's that I had a bit of a tough time following Arsenal in my formative years, they would have an inward chuckle. My first vivid Arsenal memories go back to our first European campaign in the autumn of 1963. Ten trophy-less years had passed to that point, so the teens of the day had a lot more to grumble about than I did. Arsenal were a team for whom goal-scoring wasn't an issue, but a porous defence ensured season after season of frustration. Billy Wright, then holder of the world record for international caps, had been the first manager appointed from outside the club in nearly forty years. The last one, Herbert Chapman, took five years to bring a trophy to Highbury, but the former England captain would not get as much time to deliver. In each of his four seasons, Wright's Arsenal slipped lower in the First Division table. Unlike Chapman he did not deliver a Cup Final appearance to suggest better would come. His dismissal in the summer of England's World Cup triumph was inevitable.

The man chosen to succeed him was certainly not predictable. Bertie Mee was the physiotherapist who had a reputation among the players as a strict disciplinarian, but was little known outside the walls of Highbury. Denis Hill-Wood, the chairman, and his board had gone back to the tried and trusted method of promotion from within established following the death of Chapman. Bertie was entrusted with repeating the achievements of Tom Whittaker, who moved from the treatment room to the manager's office, and delivered two League Championships and an FA Cup in a five-year spell around the start of the 50's. The new boss would be the first to acknowledge that he needed help with the coaching as the modern day game was taking shape, and the old fashioned 'trainers' now needed to develop greater tactical and motivational skills in their armoury. The appointment of the progressive Dave Sexton was a good one, and it was no surprise that he would soon go onto the 'big job' at Chelsea and Manchester United.

Fate also delivered Mee, a second lieutenant, who would get to the very top of the coaching tree. Don Howe was a former England right-back recruited by Wright, but had fallen victim to a broken leg in March from which he would not recover sufficiently to resume playing. He was a leader and a thinker who learned very quickly from the more experienced Sexton and when the latter took over at Chelsea, little over a year later Don became the chief coach of Arsenal. The gift of timing did not just present the new boss with top coaching staff. The junior set-up established by his predecessor meant that a very talented group of youngsters were graduating at much the same time. Bob Wilson, Peter Storey, Peter Simpson, George Armstrong, Jon Sammels, and John Radford were all progressing from being good prospects to established players. They were to be followed by an equally talented trio of Eddie Kelly, Charlie George, and Ray Kennedy.

Almost immediately, Bertie took the opportunity to ease out some of the established stars at the club. It is probably fair to say that the supporters were not best pleased when George Eastham and Joe Baker were shipped out to Stoke City and Nottingham Forest respectively. The two had made the initial England World Cup squad, although Baker would not survive the final cut, and many considered the best of a bad bunch had been lost. The experience that was lost was soon replaced. Although the roles vacated by Eastham and Baker would offer opportunities to Sammels and Radford, the signing of left-back Bob McNab provided a first-class solution to an old problem area. Radford, promoted from a right wing position that did not play to his strengths, would get some support up front from Scotland international George Graham, signed from Chelsea.

Proof of progress was delivered in the first season of the new regime, as Arsenal climbed from a fourteenth place finish in 1966, to seventh place twelve months on. With the benefit of hindsight it is apparent that George Graham in particular had learned the lessons of promoting the youngsters and adding the experience they lacked. Nobody at that time could have imagined what he would achieve little more than twenty years later following that train of thought.

In his second season at the helm Bertie delivered a Wembley final. It was only the second time the culmination of the League Cup had been staged at the home of English football, and we were in it. Standing between Arsenal and the trophy were a Leeds United team being honed by Don Revie. They were ruthless, and although the likes of Frank McLintock and Peter Storey matched them kick for kick, a hotly disputed volley from left-back Terry Cooper settled the match. That it was put past goalkeeper, Jim Furnell, who had been floored at a corner by big Jack Charlton, still rankles with older Gooners today.

Twelve months on an even more painful defeat would be suffered at the same stage of the same competition, and in the same place. A year earlier I had missed out on seeing my first Wembley final in the flesh. At least defeat to Leeds meant I would be present to see us grab the trophy from the frail challenge presented by Swindon Town, then in the Third Division. That was the theory, anyway. One hundred and twenty minutes of pure footballing theatre on a mud-bath (created by holding the Horse of the Year Show on the hallowed turf) left this twelve-year-old with a pain I had not experienced before, but one that would become repeated many times over in the ensuing years. Swindon were deserving winners after extra-time, but I was not as charitable at the time. Would Arsenal ever win anything in my lifetime? I was taking it very personally.

Taking it even more personally was Frank McLintock. Prior to joining Arsenal he had been in the Leicester City side that had reached two FA Cup Finals, only to lose both. That he was now a four-time runner-up left him with a burning desire to get his hands on a winner's medal. Arsenal's fourth place finish in the League was impressive, but Frank was after something better. That League position earned Arsenal a second crack at the Fairs Cup, and in Europe, as the '60's became the '70's, Mee's Arsenal came of age. A remarkable journey for the Gunners opened with a 3-1 aggregate victory over Northern Ireland's Glentoran; continued past Sporting Lisbon (3-0); Rouen (1-0); Dinamo Bacau (9-1); and Ajax (3-1) to a Final meeting with Anderlecht. To put that battering of Ajax in perspective, the Cruyff-inspired Dutchmen would go on to own the European Cup for the next three seasons. Beating them 3-0 at Highbury in the first-leg of that semi-final was probably the performance that convinced that Arsenal team they were a match for anybody on their day. Success again looked to be out of Arsenal's grasp in the first leg of the Final as the Belgian hosts took a three goal advantage, but a late header from young substitute Ray Kennedy provided the all important away goal. At a packed Highbury six days later I was on the back step of a crammed Clock End to witness fabulous strikes from Eddie Kelly and Jon Sammels – either side of a typical John Radford header – give us the trophy. Thousands streamed onto the Highbury turf to celebrate with the players daft enough to attempt a lap of honour. Bob Wilson eventually returned to the changing room stripped of everything but his dignity.

In a corner somewhere, Bertie Mee was already planning the next momentous campaign. Ray Kennedy had made six appearances in 1969-70. It is doubtful he expected to make many more in the season that followed. Fate can be as spectacularly giving as it is sometimes fickle. On the opening day at Goodison Park Charlie George broke his ankle as he scored in a 2-2 draw. The nineteen-year-old Kennedy found himself promoted as a regular starting partner to John Radford, and the pair terrorised defences as Arsenal rampaged through the opening half of the season. West Bromwich Albion were hit for six, and four goals were notched against Manchester United, Ipswich Town, Nottingham Forest, Everton, and in the Fairs Cup, Beveren Waas. Those who later called that team 'functional' conveniently overlook such performances. The team and supporters were enjoying some exciting days.

It was off the pitch that two events that would create a special bond in the team occurred. At a post-match dinner in Rome the Arsenal party reacted to an attack on Ray Kennedy in the street by going toe to toe with the players and officials of Lazio. Ten days later a hastily arranged team meeting followed a five-nil defeat at Stoke, and harsh words were encouraged as the players got that performance out of their system. That meeting owed as much to McLintock as it did to Mee and Howe. The players took responsibility and the reaction was astonishing. After that reverse in the Potteries on 26th September, Arsenal did not lose a League match for nearly four months, when a penalty awarded for a handball offence outside the area by McLintock presented Huddersfield with an unlikely triumph. The Championship was turning into a two-horse race between the Gunners and their old adversaries, Revie's Leeds. At one point in February we trailed the Yorkshiremen by seven points, the equivalent of ten today as there were only two points awarded for a win. Slowly, we reeled them in. The last thirteen League matches provided only one reverse, ironically at Leeds to another hotly disputed goal. As for the rest, there was one draw and eleven wins, six of which were by the only goal of the game. I still recall the absolute joy that followed those single goals. In particular Charlie George's belligerent thump from the edge of the box to beat Newcastle, and Eddie Kelly's spectacular finish to avenge our battering at Stoke. It was of course the last match of that nerve-jangling sequence that provided yet more unforgettable moments, and another single-goal drama.

So, a decade after Tottenham lifted the first double of the twentieth century they were all that stood between FA Cup finalists Arsenal, and the first leg of what would become the second. A year after a late header in Belgium set us up for a Fairs Cup triumph, Ray Kennedy was to repeat the achievement at a packed White Hart Lane, where at least as many as got in the ground were locked outside. Not bad for a nineteen-year-old who must have thought he would spend the season in the reserves. It was absolutely brilliant for a fourteen-year-old Arsenal fanatic savouring every moment of it on the Shelf. The margin between success and failure is sometimes minute indeed, and the resilience shown by the men in red as they repelled the Spurs onslaught that followed that goal paled into insignificance five days later at Wembley. Chances came and went as Arsenal missed the opportunity to do the second leg of the double in ninety minutes against Bill Shankly's Liverpool. In the opening minute of the added half hour Bob Wilson made an uncharacteristic error of judgement, and we were a goal down on a very hot and strength-sapping afternoon. If I could convey one thing about the Arsenal of this era, I would like it to be the strength they showed in adversity. The spirit of determination instilled into the side by a combination of Mee's discipline, Howe's persuasive powers, and McLintock's sheer bloody-minded never give up attitude, was quite awesome. Eddie Kelly's equaliser and Charlie George's unforgettable winner produced a turnaround of epic proportions. The hat I had trodden into the Wembley terracing after Liverpool's opener was retrieved, bashed back into shape, and planted proudly back on my head for the lap of honour. The pain of two years earlier was banished, but only temporarily. The next of many more Final disappointments was just twelve months away, and it was dirty Leeds again.

The aftermath of the double was more significant than any of us perhaps realised at the time. Don Howe left Highbury to manage his former club, West Bromwich Albion. As he himself remarked on the Official History of Arsenal DVD, "There's been times when I left that I should have stayed. The double time was one of those when I left, and I should have stayed, because there was a lot more in that team." Indeed there should have been. Not that it was immediately apparent to those of us on the terraces that the best of the era had come and gone. The following Christmas we signed Alan Ball, a World Cup winner, from Everton for a British record fee of £220,000. Ball's strength was his quick one touch passing game, somewhat at odds with Arsenal's desire to get the ball wide and cross for the big men. The champions suffered twelve defeats and yet finished only six points behind their successors, Derby County. A year later we finished as runners-up, just three points behind Liverpool, and reached the semi-final of the FA Cup, only to lose to Second Division Sunderland, who went on to defeat Leeds at Wembley.

The break up of the side started with George Graham's sale to Manchester United when Ball arrived. In the summer of 1973 the skipper, McLintock, was sold to Queens Park Rangers, much to his surprise. A year later Ray Kennedy became Bill Shankly's last signing for Liverpool and Bob Wilson retired. By the close of the 1974/5 season, Arsenal had returned to the bottom half of the table, surviving relegation by four points. Bob McNab moved to Wolverhampton Wanderers and, most shockingly for the supporters, Charlie George turned down the overtures of Tottenham and was shipped out to Derby in his prime. Four years after winning the double, half of a great side was elsewhere. Next out of the door, twelve months later, was Bertie himself after just six points separated us from the drop. Although Mee's tenure had gone full cycle, from bust to boom to bust, what he achieved around the turn of the decade persuaded the board to continue to appoint men with an Arsenal background to the managerial hot seat. Next up was Terry Neill, captain of the club in Mee's early days, and a man who maintained a close relationship with the club chairman, Dennis Hill-Wood. Initially Neill found the job quite a challenge. The Arsenal dressing room had contained strong characters for some time. When Alan Hudson and Malcolm Macdonald were added to Alan

Ball, the new manager frequently found his authority challenged. The time had come to recall Don Howe.

Neill, like Mee before him, had inherited some remarkable young talent, and once again good timing presented him with David O'Leary, Liam Brady, and Frank Stapleton, all approaching their peak years. Slowly, the old heads were moved on, and a vibrant side took shape around the talented Irish trio. Macdonald survived the cuts, but sadly not a dodgy knee. With Howe at his side, Neill turned things around to such an extent that Arsenal reached three consecutive FA Cup Finals, and their second European Final, in the Cup Winners Cup. That only one of those was won remains a mystery to this day. That Arsenal side should have achieved more, and probably would have done had two of the leading lights not have been lured away. Like the double side a decade earlier, the keystones of the side were lost. Liam Brady had been open about his desire to test himself at the highest level: in those days that meant Italy. In the wake of our double Final defeats in 1980, Liam joined Juventus, where he would win back-to-back Serie A titles. More controversially Stapleton departed for a huge pay rise at Old Trafford a year later. Within eighteen months Neill was also heading for the exit door, having failed to adequately replace the two Irishmen and Macdonald's goals. Don Howe finally moved up to the big job, but later reflected that this was the time he stayed at Arsenal when perhaps he should have left. He lasted slightly over two years and left when it became known that Arsenal had offered his job to Terry Venables. That was the closest that the club came to bringing in another 'outsider' until the appointment of Bruce Rioch in 1995.

When Venables turned the club down, George Graham, a double-winner under Bertie Mee, returned to Highbury as manager in May 1986. Like his old boss before him, he cleared out what was perceived to be the old guard and promoted a fine crop of youngsters, added some quality and experience from elsewhere, and instilled a degree of discipline and spirit that brought the club another spell of success. That blueprint yielded almost immediate rewards. Graham became the first Arsenal manager to land the previously cursed League Cup in 1987 when an Ian Rush strike was overturned by two goals from Charlie Nicholas. Although Luton would heap more misery on Arsenal supporters in the Final a year later, Graham was slowly bringing together possibly the most talented group of young players the club has known, and supplementing them from shrewd signings from clubs large and small. League championships were secured in 1989 and 1991 with a side famed for defensive impregnability, but like the side in 1971 it didn't really get the credit it deserved as an exhilarating attacking force on occasion. Like their illustrious predecessors, Graham's Gunners too developed a strong team bond. That 'us against the world' mentality meant the side could overcome the deduction of two points in their second title-winning season. Only Chelsea at Stamford Bridge prevented Arsenal from going an entire League season unbeaten that term.

The arrival of Ian Wright heralded an era where the club once again impressed predominantly in cup competitions. In 1993 Arsenal became the first club to land the domestic cup double, defeating Sheffield Wednesday at Wembley in both. A year later European glory was tasted for the second time when a much-weakened Gunners side ground out a single goal triumph against Cup-Winners Cup holders Parma. If you had mentioned to those of us who enjoyed the intoxicating atmosphere of Copenhagen that George would be gone within a year we would have laughed at the suggestion. In truth though his powers were already on the wane, and his transfer dealings would provide the ammunition to fire him so controversially.

As with Bertie Mee, it could be argued that George struggled to rebuild his best side. When you consider his first five signings were Groves, Smith, Winterburn, Richardson, and Dixon, whilst his last five were McGoldrick, Schwartz, Hartson, Kiwomya, and Helder, perhaps that viewpoint is easy to appreciate. That doesn't detract from the pleasure and success both brought to supporters who had been deprived of silverware for a long time. The Mee blueprint was cast aside with George's departure. Bruce Rioch was recruited from Bolton, and lasted but a year before Arsene Wenger was handed the reins. In these days of huge television contracts, huge wages, and massive commercialism, it is doubtful anybody would take the risk of appointing from within. Big clubs these days demand big name managers, rightly or wrongly. However it is hard to deny that having a degree of continuity, and trusting the management of the club to men who understood what it was all about from the inside, was a demonstrably successful approach for almost sixty years.

David Faber, otherwise known as Goonerholic, was born eleven months after Liam Brady, and therefore arrived at a time when all the footballing genius for the era had been exhausted. He has quietly followed Arsenal home and away ever since.

20

STAN KROENKE – INVESTOR TO OWNER IN 5 YEARS

TIM PAYTON

My first sight of Stan Kroenke wasn't what I was expecting. Having been chaperoned through *Claridge's* by a porter up to one of the hotel's premium suites, I was ushered into the office area of a large apartment. And there was Stan, resplendent from head-to-toe in his Arsenal tracksuit. Sitting alongside him was his son, Josh, now President of their basketball team, The Denver Nuggets, also decked out in Arsenal gear. As a representative of the Arsenal Supporters' Trust (AST) calling by to find out more about what Stan thought about Arsenal, I felt underdressed in my business suit devoid of any cannons, red or white.

It was Spring 2007 and the meeting had a certain clandestine element to it. For this was the time when the Arsenal Board still weren't talking to Stan Kroenke. He might by then have owned 12% of Arsenal Holdings

PLC but the club's Chairman and board had at that stage decided that they didn't wish to engage. The AST took a different view. We had written to Stan as soon as his purchase of ITV's 9.99% stake in the club was announced. We were ready because his decision to buy a stake in Arsenal hadn't exactly come as a surprise. Arsenal had entered into a business partnership with his MLS club, the Colorado Rapids. Initially, this was presented as a tie-up based on sharing best practice on marketing know-how, football development and stadia expertise (the Rapids were finalising their own plans for what is now Dick's Sporting Goods Park). But to all seasoned watchers it made sense that there was more to it than this.

This was the period when the first wave of American businessmen were looking to invest in Premier League clubs recognising, that while the US might lead the world in sports business expertise, and it was English football that possessed the must watch content the world wanted to see. The Glazers, Randy Lerner, and Hicks & Gillette were all already settling into their ownership of other major Premier League clubs.

Nick Harris, a leading British sports journalist with strong contacts in the States, had initially brought Kroenke's interest in Arsenal to the attention of the public. He broke the story of the tie-up between Kroenke Sports Enterprises (KSE) and Arsenal in the Independent newspaper on 7th of February 2007 and suggested that the relationship might

soon develop as ITV were actively seeking to sell their holding. So the AST was not surprised when it was announced
on 7th of April 2007 that ITV had sold their 9.99 per cent
stake in Arsenal for £42m together with a further £23m for
their 50 per cent holding in Arsenal Broadband Limited,
a separate arm of Arsenal that controls the club's media
rights and internet business.

The AST wrote to Stan Kroenke welcoming him to
Arsenal and expressing a wish to work together for the
good of the club. It has been a philosophy of the AST since
our foundation that all major shareholders and supporter
groups should work together to take Arsenal forward. It
is proven in football that stability off the pitch creates an
environment for success on it. In this period we met regularly not only with Arsenal board members but also with
ITV and other shareholders – including the hedge fund
Lansdowne Partners. Our initial assessment was that Stan
Kroenke's experience in property development, sports marketing and TV rights, would be a positive addition to the
skillsets at the club at that time.

We received a swift response which was the first ever
public statement made by Stan Kroenke on his involvement in Arsenal, recorded in full below for the first time:

*Dear Tim, thank you very much for your thoughtful letter and
constructive support for our investment in the Club. Everyone*

at Kroenke Sports Enterprises is proud to be associated with Arsenal both through this investment and the marketing and commercial agreement between Arsenal and the Colorado Rapids.

We have made a significant investment in football in the US both in stadium facilities for the expanded MLS (major soccer league) as well as player, training and coaching facilities to support the general development of the sport nationally at all levels. I see major long-term potential for football and have made a strong commitment to its development.

Incidentally Keith Edelman, Adrian Ford and Amanda Docherty kindly joined us in Denver this past Saturday for the very successful opening of our new MLS stadium and 24 adjacent youth fields.

I recognise and appreciate the AST role and contribution to the Club and the valuable perspective which you provide to the shareholders, board and management. Over the next months I look forward to learning more about the club through a dialogue with you all. This will inform a view about how our investment can support Arsenal. In closing, we are extremely happy with our relationship and investment in Arsenal. We much admire the values and culture of the Club.

I look forward to meeting you and the other members of the Arsenal family over the next months.

Kindest regards,
Stan Kroenke

The dialogue continued and a few weeks later came a call from one of his advisers. "Stan would like to meet," they said. So it was off to *Claridge's* where he had just returned from incognito tour of the club's Armoury shop – which explained why one of the richest men in American greeted me in an Arsenal tracksuit. We spoke for more than an hour, about Arsenal, about KSE, and mainly about the ownership structure at Arsenal and boardroom politics at Arsenal where Stan was on the beginning of a steep learning curve. He had more questions for me than I was able to put to him. It felt like being a part of the due diligence he was undertaking and he was naturally keen to learn more about the Supporters' Trust and our observations on the how the club was run. Including why David Dein, who had courted his involvement in the club once his initial interest had been known, had subsequently been dismissed from the Board and marched out of the club when the sale of ITV's shares to Kroenke was announced.

It was the first of several warm and friendly meetings with Stan. Since then, and over the years, many people have asked me what Stan is like. The answer is 'not like you'd expect', and not reflective of the 'Silent Stan' moniker he have been given as a result of avoiding both the media and public platforms. Far from being silent, he is a warm, gregarious host, who enjoys conversation and telling stories. Yes he owns lots of sports teams and can relate the recent scores and performances of all of them, but it doesn't take long to discern that the Denver Nuggets are to him what the Arsenal is to me – his true sporting love. I soon learnt to look up the latest news on the likely trade of Allen Iverson or how the Nuggets were faring in their battle to make the play-offs to really bring the conversation to life.

On Arsenal he was refreshingly honest. He didn't claim to have been a fan for life and wasn't going to pretend he had; all the better in my view for not attempting to reel off a list of badly pronounced members of the Cup winning team from Copenhagen 1994 to try and prove some undying bond. Instead he spoke of his strategic interest in English football and explained that he had been approached with several offers and opportunities to get involved with many teams from England but that once he saw Arsenal he felt the club had values and attributes that struck a chord with his own. He also stressed his wider commitment to 'soccer' through the investment he was making into the Colorado Rapids.

In reality this means that he saw the potential of a club that had recently moved into a brand new 60,000 stadium in the centre of London. He said had become a fan after a process of observation and involvement including watching games at the newly-built Emirates, incognito with the paying punters. The team then was garnering world-wide acclaim for the football being played under Arsene Wenger, whom Stan spoke of with the complete respect and reverence – even joking that he wished he could borrow his services to help out some of his other teams.

Over time as he got to know the club's set-up, finances and playing personnel better our occasional conversations turned to us asking him questions and what I'd term football fan lingo. I recall some banter with him where he readily agreed that watching Manuel Almunia keep goal was a nerve-wracking experience and it was clear that he followed the team's matches closely albeit from long distance. Our prompting that he should come to Arsenal on match-days themselves, so he could get a feel for the club and its fans, was met with an explanation of how difficult it was to be everywhere at once given the size of business interests he was running. It was a relationship that myself and AST colleagues were to develop over the next couple years, including a visit later that summer to Colorado, to sharing a beer at the Diamond Club bar during the AST Christmas drinks.

The visit to Denver was invaluable for giving us a far greater insight into Stan and the sports business empire he was constructing. Fellow AST board member Nigel Phillips and I were given a whirlwind tour of meetings and discussions led by then KSE Chief Operating Officer Paul Andrews and Colorado Rapids Chief executive Jeff Plush – with the highlight being a visit to see Colorado Rapids beat FC Dallas by two goals to one. It was a match with Arsenal interest on both sides. Steve Morrow was managing Dallas that day and Gary Smith had joined the Rapids from Arsenal, becoming their first team coach (later to become manager and lead them to the MLS Cup in 2010).

By the time we arrived the Arsenal influence could be spotted in several small ways. A section of the Rapid's home stadium had been renamed 'Cannon's Corner' and it housed an actual cannon that was fired when the Rapids scored. There was a choice of Arsenal home and away shirts in the club shop and a global map in the front office with Arsenal, London highlighted. There were also extensive youth football facilities and plans for an Arsenal Academy.

During our visit, the AST was introduced to many of the senior executives of KSE and had a presentation from Paul Andrews on the business plan. It was explained to us that Kroenke Sports Enterprises (KSE) saw themselves as the Rocky Mountain West's leading provider of live sports and entertainment events. Based in Denver, KSE is a privately held company owned by Stan Kroenke that operates Denver's Pepsi Center arena, sports franchises and presenting live entertainment events. More than 3 million fans annually experience professional sports and entertainment through KSE. In addition to the Colorado Rapids and a separate interest in the NFL's St Louis Rams, the KSE sports teams are, the Colorado Avalanche, a National Hockey League team who moved to Denver from Quebec in 1995 and has since won two Stanley Cups; The Denver Nuggets, Colorado's National Basketball Association representative for more than 25 years and the oldest NBA team in the mountain states region; Colorado Mammoth, Denver's indoor Lacrosse team play at the Pepsi Centre and won the NLL title in 2006; the Colorado Rapids and the Colorado Crush who play indoor Arena Football – an indoor, small-sized version of the NFL which didn't particularly grip Nigel when he took in a game.

We were informed that KSE operated under the corporate tag 'Memories are played here' with a mission statement that reads:

Kroenke Sports Enterprises is committed to providing world class sports and entertainment for both live and broadcast audiences. We will welcome fans into our venues as family, providing respect and care from the purchase of a ticket, to the drive home. We will celebrate the best in sport and entertainment by recognising the diversity and human spirit around us, and by working within our community to improve the lives of all those within the community.

Our visit also allowed us to see the emphasis placed by KSE on commercial revenues, driven by ticket sales and the sports television station, Altitude. Altitude is a regional sports network for the Nuggets, Avalanche, Mammoth and Rapids. The channel is an important marketing and branding tool for KSE's sports teams and distributes sports coverage across the United States on satellite and regional TV.

We certainly saw evidence that demonstrated no stone was left unturned in the commercial application of KSE's sports teams, driven by an emphasis on service quality and excellence, and the importance the club places on its links to supporters and the local community. It was also clear just how different US sports are to those in England and the different expectation of the supporters. It was noticeable that there was as great an emphasis on the supporters 'match-day' experience as well as the team's actual performance. Something the Emirates has sought to replicate with a focus on 'Arsenalisation'. Many of those we met in Denver spoke well of Stan, but admitted that they had never met him and reiterated his preference for keeping a low profile and letting their sports teams do the talking.

In the round, we saw that KSE was about building a sports portfolio business that serviced itself through ticket sales, commercial revenues and broadcasting rights. This was a long-term endeavour with commercial benefit secured through asset growth. Adding an English Premier League team to the mix was the logical next stage in the expansion, alongside Kroenke taking full ownership of the St Louis Rams.

As Jeff Plush, who had previously had responsibility for spearheading KSE's strategic business initiatives, new media enterprises and brand development, explained, "This ground-breaking alliance with Arsenal, a team that has been in the first flights of the sport for more than 100 years, is the one of the stepping stones to continue pushing our sport into the next level. In today's international business community, soccer is the only true global sport that transcends ethnicity, culture and language and with this type of relationship we are making sure that our company is expanding this vision through worldwide sport."

One big difference we saw was the focus, and effort, put by KSE into selling tickets for matches. KSE teams have a business model driven by an emphasis on ticket sales that ranges from sixty to eighty-percent of revenue across the teams. Banks of sales executives were executing ticketing strategies that included season tickets, mini plan sales, group sales and single game strategy. With Denver hosting many sports teams in a relatively low population area, this is a necessary factor. Of course Arsenal have for many years had little need for such actions, as 42,000 people sign over a year's money on June 1st each year, and while demand has softened, there is still a waiting list for both club level and general admission season tickets

In more recent times the AST's dialogue with Stan Kroenke has waned. Perhaps not surprisingly as in this time he joined the Arsenal Board and his energies would have been diverted toward spending time getting to know the other directors and learning more about Arsenal's business before launching his takeover offer in the early summer of 2011.

The AST did urge him, and still do so – in fact more than ever – to speak up and talk to fans, believing that his words will be well received. Saying nothing only fuels concern and mistrust. His silence before the takeover was often explained on the grounds that to say anything on his intentions would fetter his freedom to make a bid. In fact, the reporting of Kroenke to the takeover panel for allegedly being in concert with Danny Fiszman led to noticeably more reticence as the lawyers got to work defending the charge.

Now, fast forward to late 2011 and although his words at the recent AGM and a couple of press briefings are encouraging, Stan hasn't really found a way to step forward and create a connection and understanding between himself and Arsenal fans that builds on some of the welcome words that were included in the formal offer document. In that document Stan Kroenke states that if he does takeover Arsenal he plans to "provide Arsenal with continued stability from an individual who not only understands and greatly respects the history and traditions of Arsenal, but who also has a proven record of successful long-term investment in sport."

He also said that he would make it a priority "to meet with supporters and fan groups in formal and informal settings and recognises that fans are at the heart of the Club. Their opinions and involvement are important to him. Mr Kroenke fully expects himself, the Arsenal Directors and Club executives to continue to engage supporters for the long-term good of the Club".

To date he hasn't really expanded in much detail on these comments or answered many of the other questions that supporters have. One thing is certain – if he doesn't communicate there will always be a sense of unease amongst Arsenal fans. A survey undertaken by the Arsenal Supporters' Trust (AST) in June 2011 found that 96% of its membership wanted Kroenke to 'improve his communications with supporters including setting out his ambitions for the club and explaining the strategy he has to achieve them'.

This doesn't necessarily mean arranging an interview with Newsnight's Jeremy Paxman, but could manifest itself through attendance at more matches and engaging with not only the AST but with other supporter's groups such as AISA and RedAction. Such action would allow information to cascade to fans via word of mouth and Arsenal's voracious social media led by sites such as Arseblog. There are also established channels such as Arsenal.com and the match-day programme where over the years the owners of Arsenal have taken the time to communicate with the club's fans.

I hope he does take this course of action and allows more fans to see the Stan Kroenke I met in 2007 – the billionaire in the Arsenal tracksuit.

Tim Payton is a board member of the Arsenal Supporter's Trust and founder member of Arsenal Fanshare.

21

GLORY DAYS

JAKE MORRIS

I had assumed it to be a love affair whose passion would never dim. Only death or the loss of faculties would, I thought, take us away from each other: Arsenal and I. For so many years nothing occupied more of my waking hours. It was never one of life's truly important things, but as Pope John Paul II apparently observed, of all the unimportant things; none is more important than football. The gap between games was always too long and the regular fortnightly international breaks seemed profoundly unfair. The summer was to be endured rather than enjoyed, the second Saturday in August such a blessed relief that even now I can recall what I was doing on the day Arsenal opened their league campaign.

United away (1-4) 1989-90: I was in the garden and Dad called out the result from inside. Wimbledon away

(3-0) 1990-91: heard on the radio in the car. QPR (1-1) 1991-92: France, on the balcony trying to get some decent reception on the World Service.

Pinpointing the beginning of the affair is not easy. A 1-1 draw at Old Trafford on 2nd April 1989 is my best guess; a Sunday afternoon at Grandma and Grandpa's; Grandpa in his big green chair nearest the TV, and me to his left. Tony Adams scored at both ends, which when you're three days past your 7th birthday is the kind of thing that sticks in your mind. There were a couple of earlier dates – Norwich at home on Bank Holiday Monday afternoon. Mum let us watch some of it and then decided we'd been in front of the TV for long enough and should go and play with our toys or something. And Derby at home – news of our shock 2-1 defeat relayed in the car by Dad as we drove past Lords Cricket Ground. And then, well, there was Anfield a fortnight later.

Come the fourth home game of the following season we were in the family enclosure for Arsenal v Manchester City to see John Lukic's long goal kick from the Clock End disappear from view (for those sitting far enough back in the west lower), before dropping back into orbit in time for Michael Thomas to stab home in front of the North Bank. And so I became obsessed. Fast-forward twenty-odd years and, as usual, I'd spent the week anticipating the visit of Wolves to the Emirates stadium. We'd drawn 1-1 at Birmingham the previous weekend, conceding a last minute equaliser in a fashion hauntingly familiar to events on the same ground two years previously in a game that had spelt the beginning of the very quick end of a title charge built up over 26 games.

Despite that 1-1 draw, we still, by most people's reckoning, had a decent stab at the title *if* we could beat Wolves. For 90 minutes we laboured. Four of the five minutes of injury time were up and it was still 0-0, then Denilson had it. "Long, long, long," I screamed, almost crazed, from my seat down by the corner flag. He didn't go long. But of all the short passes in his Arsenal career (and there were a few), this turned out to be one of the better ones because when Bacary Sagna eventually crossed, Nicklas Bendtner squeezed his header into the corner of the net and people sunk to their knees and thanked the heavens. I was one of those people. Rarely, in my two and a bit decades of watching Arsenal had I seen a single league goal greeted with such an outpouring of emotion. On that night I went to the pub with Arsenal supporting friends and agreed and disagreed about whether we were talking about Arsenal too much, or as much as we ever had in all our time watching the club. I imagined we'd do the same for decades to come. But two weeks later something changed and that, really, is the point of this piece.

When we went to Wigan, our chance of the title wasn't great but it was still a lot more likely than it had ever been at any point for Liverpool or Spurs over the previous years.

Watching the game meant making my excuses early at a gathering of my girlfriend's family, so on a cloudless spring afternoon, I sat in an almost deserted home-counties pub, eyes fixed on a television. My thinking: if I thought we could still win the title, it was not a lot to ask for the players to think the same and give it a proper go. But that day, Arsenal didn't. Going 2-0 up was celebrated with about as much seriousness as the same score would elicit in a testimonial. The subsequent conceding of three goals in the final ten minutes, turning victory into defeat, would have been pretty alarming even in such a game. When I left the pub that day and joined my girlfriend for a walk along the canal towpath in the last of that afternoon's light, I knew something had changed.

Even when we'd lost 6-1 at Old Trafford a decade earlier, I'd have rather seen the game than not seen it. But now, for the first time ever, a part of me actually regretted watching Arsenal that day. Since that Wigan day it has never been the same; I know it hasn't.

A year after the Wolves game, the Emirates witnessed another incredible finish. Arsenal v Liverpool was 0-0 after 95 minutes, 1-0 after 96 minutes and 1-1 after 97 minutes. No less an emotional rollercoaster than the Wolves match and yet I watched it with a sense of detachment. Among the same friends, as obsessed as I, the same feeling is true. We miss far more games than we once did. We can sit through someone's birthday lunch without checking the score every five minutes, with ease. But how is this possible and why now?

A part of me wonders if perhaps on that day in Wigan the contract between player and fan was completely broken. I had never considered it an equal relationship; I'd commit not just my time and money but also vast amounts of emotion and an arguably unhealthy degree of worship for individual players. In return I don't think I'd expected too much. I didn't expect them to play well *every* game and I'm not particularly picky about what they are like as people. That said, when Arsenal have been linked with one or two players whose lives and criminal history are impossible to plead ignorance to, I've not wanted us to sign them, on the premise that I know too much for the necessary suspension of belief to occur. My point here is that when you think you're watching hugely well-paid footballers frankly *not* trying, that same thing can happen.

In the beginning the idea appears almost so fanciful that you are prepared to believe it is one's own ignorance of the game that is to blame for gaining such an impression. However, when you see the games like the one at Wigan, alarm bells ring. When former players, who know what they're talking about, start saying what you're thinking about the effort or lack of it, those bells ring louder. That day at Wigan, they didn't give 100%. The truth is there had been games before and there have been games since when the same has been true. The commitment of

Arsene Wenger is unarguable but whether his charges are still prepared to fight for him is less apparent. It is their fault but in a sense his problem. That would be the easy explanation.

Another explanation is growing up and getting married, although I struggle to buy this completely. I was probably in the top 1% of football obsessives. I planned my life around Arsenal. I watched (in person, television or the internet) every single game. I've blogged about the club for seven years, spending many hundreds, if not thousands of hours, doing so. I can even date most family holidays and birthdays by cross referencing who we played that day, who scored the goals and therefore what the year must be. So how, put crudely, could women be to blame? I don't think the fact that I am missing more games *per se* is of too great an importance. I'm missing games for the same reasons that I always missed games. The difference is that nowadays there are more such incidents. So, for example the Jewish New Year (which always seems to coincide with Arsenal matches) forced me to miss the Olympiakos match this year, just as I had missed the first leg of OB Odense v Arsenal for the same reason 18 years previously. Only when the crunch game with United in spring 2003 clashed with Passover was it considered appropriate to leave the festival dinner table.

Work makes me miss games too, but none of that explains why I'm not checking the score as avidly as I did before, or why I am not churning the result over in mind time and time again. Then there is a third, more frightening scenario: am I simply less interested because we're just no longer as good as we once were? For all my obsessiveness over the years, am I no better than the proverbial glory hunter? On Friday 16th April 2004, I had a pre-match drink with a friend in a pub near Highbury before the Leeds game. That friend never, ever drank before a game, but so confident was he that nothing could stop our march to the title, he allowed himself a pint. As he drank it, he said: "Enjoy this, because we'll never have it so good again." They were serious words from a 21 year-old but he had a point. Thierry Henry scored four goals that night and in the stands people turned and looked at each other in wonderment as every dance through the Leeds defence became more outrageous. We became The Invincibles and for nine games the following season we were even better. When Villa came to Highbury for game number 49; the absence of Freddie Ljungberg and Gilberto Silva forced Wenger into picking what, at that brief time in Autumn 2004, was not his first team but was his very best team. Against mid-rate opposition at Highbury, the creativity of a very young Fabregas was of more use alongside Patrick Vieira than Gilberto's defensive wall. Jose Reyes was in the (very brief) peak of his Arsenal career, terrorising defences and knocking in goals with his left foot, right foot and head. Villa, despite enjoying an early lead, were destroyed.

The Clock End enquired whether our opponents had "ever seen football played like this" and there is, I think, a part of me that did become spoilt. Football in the late '90's and early '00's at Arsenal became something a little bit different to most football. Yes, like football fans at any level of the game, we were thrilled by the odd seesaw encounter or controversial moment. Yes, it goes without saying, the reason the Premier League is so popular is – relatively speaking – the football is superior to many other leagues.

It goes without saying that the great Arsenal sides of the time never did win the Champions League, nor did they manage back-to-back league titles, but it is true that we would regularly be treated to moments that we could simply not conceive. It was as if we were at the finest of restaurants where the boundaries were continually being pushed. At the heart of it was Thierry Henry, an extraordinary innovator. I sat in a pub in Camden Town watching our home game with Charlton in Autumn 2004 on mute, when Henry scored *that* back-heeled goal. It was the goal that was actually too clever for the camera. Viewers were treated to a close up of the man with his back to goal but no goal in shot. The vision mixer presumably, like the rest of us, simply couldn't imagine a goal could be scored from that position. It did become, I think, a little bit about having your breath taken away. Of course there were football matches to win. I've acknowledged we never came close to matching Manchester United's consistency over many seasons. All the same, it is true that once a game was won or ever appeared likely to be won, it was no longer enough to simply score normal goals; at least certainly not in Henry's mind. They had to be beautifully crafted. If need be, the easy option had to be passed up if the more difficult one was visually better. Sod the goal difference. Part of going to Arsenal became about those moments you got a few times a game, moments that would stir something inside you in a way not a lot else could.

Even when The Invincibles broke up, Henry was still around for a while longer; Cesc was there, RVP was there and Arshavin and then Nasri signed too. But, as we knew while having that drink before the Leeds game in 2004, it could never be as good as it was forever. Technically, the players who now constitute the bulk of the current squad are not bad players. In fact, they are by and large very good players, but it is not uncommon to go through a game now and not once experience a moment of breathtaking beauty or execution when compared to what used to be on offer. That is not to say there aren't any. The ingenuity of Robin Van Persie's equaliser against Barcelona at the Emirates in February 2011 or indeed the slick passing that led to Andrei Arshavin's winner were two such occasions.

Arshavin had an open goal to aim at when scoring against Swansea in September 2011, but the way he nonchalantly swept the ball first time with his left foot at a tiny angle evoked memories of the arrogant strut that character-ised Arsene Wenger's greatest sides.

There is a simple truth; when football teams are not suc-cessful, fewer people follow them or come to watch them play. That is unarguable and is it fair to say that perhaps it is the case that a very great number of football fans are glory hunters. Maybe I am just one of them, hooked by Anfield, retained by a continual diet of trophies and now they're no longer assured my passion is somewhat diminished. Of course, the kind of football obsessiveness where one thinks of little else other than football is not confined to younger fans; my original assumption was probably very naive. That one's degree of obsessiveness should stay constant forever, not buffeted by the rest of life's events, was never likely. I now realise that there is, in all likelihood, an alternative; one where football is still really, really important but doesn't quite evoke the rawness of emotion it once did.

Having put to paper my thoughts, I now suspect my experience is very common. Maybe it is only because of my previous level of obsessiveness that I am so aware of something that others probably take in their stride. Why it is happening now rather than why it is happening at all is perhaps the question. This is where the factors I've out-lined above come in. That my life is changing undoubtedly has played a part, but it is also true that at times the Arsenal of late have made it easier not to obsess over them. Finally, Arsenal are no longer The Invincibles and the fact is The

Invincibles cast one almighty shadow. One really, really, really didn't want to miss an opportunity to see them. Comparatively, any team looks less attractive.

Maybe that is glory hunting. But it is at least honest.

Jake Morris started following Arsenal four games before Anfield 1989. Over 20 years of obsession later, he wonders why Arsenal now doesn't matter quite as much as he did. He has written www.goodplaya.com since September 2004.

22

FROM CHAMP TO CHAMPIGNON

JONATHAN SWAN

In the 1985/86 season, Niall Quinn loped into Sunday Mass at a local church in Enfield, North London. This caused a mini riot, as he was with a certain 'Champagne' Charlie Nicholas. Whether Chas was wearing his black leather suit, history neglects to tell, but eyewitnesses on the day remember that although the young girls there had eyes only for Bonny Prince Charlie and his regal mullet, the older ladies of the parish were drawn to the gangling Niall; because the largely Irish congregation knew that big Quinny was one of the last of his kind; the authentic Irish Arsenal player. And how. Hilariously, while an apprentice at Arsenal, Quinn claimed to have lodged with a couple of lads called Pat and Mick. Could his emerald bona get any more fide?

What Niall represented was a tail end of an era that had, at one point, seen Highbury resembling the arrivals hall of the Fishguard ferry. Throughout the 1970's Arsenal's ranks had been swollen with Irishmen from North and South. What drew them? As Kevin Costner observed in Field of Dreams, 'If you build it, they will come,' but in this case it appeared less of a deliberate policy and more of a happy accident, akin to realising you've somehow accumulated five ornamental eggcups, so you might as well start collecting them properly.

Arsenal had always had a smattering of Irish players, like Dr Kevin O' Flanagan (the flying Doctor, perhaps?) who played on the wing for the club post WWII; Joe Haverty, Paddy Sloan and Jimmy Dunne, who played in the title winning side of the 1930's. In fact, most English clubs had the odd Scot, Irish or Welshman knocking about, and that was about as exotic as it got. If you had predicted back then that an Arsenal team containing Africans, Frenchmen and South Americans would one day win the league, you would, frankly, have been regarded as a madman. Arsenal were no different to other clubs; until the Irish invasion proper began in the 1960's with Terry Neill and Arsene's faithful consigliore, Pat Rice in the vanguard. Nowadays, you can imagine Pat at the team BBQ, flipping the steaks and sucking on a beer while Arsene holds court from a shaded wicker chair with a glass of Bordeaux.

Soon came the others. In no particular order: Sammy Nelson, a left back with the most famous underpants in first division football after he dropped his shorts to the North

Bank; David O'Leary, still the record appearance holder for the club; Frank Stapleton, a classy striker whose departure to Manchester United left a bitter taste; Liam Brady, a genius of a player who was genuinely world class; St Patrick of Jennings who, despite joining from Spurs, found his way into Arsenal fan's affections; and John Devine, who filled in for Rice and had a few runs in the first team.

By the mid 1970s Arsenal could (and did) field a line up which contained six or seven Irish lads, from North and South. London in the 1970s could be no fun for your average Irishman abroad. The troubles were in full swing and anyone with an Irish accent could find themselves the focus of unwelcome attention if anything went wrong (and often if it didn't). But none of this really impinged on the Arsenal. We just got on with being a not relegated, but not really troubling the upper half of the table sort of team, while northerners took the league every year. There wasn't a particularly Irish vibe about the place either. Oddly enough, quite a lot of kids with Irish parents were Spurs fans, which may have had more to do with the quasi-religious attraction of Pat Jennings than anything else. Has any man carried off a halo and sideburns so well?

None of the Arsenal players were particularly in the public eye, either. Charlie George, our baddest boy (put your hand down at the back, Mr Storey), had gone by 1975, and few, if any, of the Irish players were especially wild. Liam Brady's biggest vice was chips, and if you had invited any of them to a roasting they would have assumed you meant chicken or lamb. The avaricious (the North Bank faithful gave it another name: rearrange these letters to find the phrase: 'creedy gunt') Frank Stapleton probably stayed in counting his money, if Tony Cascarino's autobiography is to be believed. Incidentally, what was Cascarino doing playing for Ireland with a name like that: surely the 'o' should have been at the other end?

Under Terry Neill, the club wasn't really doing much – we just drifted along. It wasn't even a deliberate ploy to have a team loaded with Irish players; it was just the way it had happened, which sort of summed us up. Some of the players we had were pretty good. Brady, obviously, was the real gem. Stapleton was a good player, and O'Leary was a cultured centre half who these days would probably command a vast fee. If Arsenal today had as many Irish players as we did back then, no doubt some marketing genius would ensure that we were maximising our revenue streams by Oirsihing us up; Guinness on tap, shamrocks on the cannon, Gunnersuarus taken out to the car park, shot and replaced by half time leprechauns, not to mention the full New York St Paddy's Day experience to draw in the punters. Perhaps a Pat Rice shebeen under the stadium selling poteen too? But really, no great fuss was made.

Even if we didn't make a big deal about our Irishness, one effect it did have was to make the Arsenal much more popular in Ireland. The dominance of Manchester United, with their glamour rep and George Best, and perennial 70's winners Liverpool just a ferry ride away, made it pretty hard for any English club to compete in attracting supporters. But Brady, especially, drew in young kids and Arsenal built up a healthy support, helped too by the fact that most of our Irish players played internationally for the Republic or Northern Ireland.

Eventually Arsenal's Irish base pretty much dispersed, over the course of our three consecutive FA Cup finals. By the 1980 final (over which a veil shall be drawn), we managed to field four Irish players (five if you include sub Sammy Nelson), but the writing was on the wall. Liam Brady was about to go to Juventus. Pat Rice was to leave for Watford only a couple of weeks later. Sammy Nelson was in the twilight of his career, and a year later Frank Stapleton would depart the marble halls, not with a fanfare of trumpets but to the jingle of the cash register. O'Leary was the only regular first teamer left. Pat Jennings, the man with the most 70's hairstyle in football, was confronted with the horrific idea that a new decade might necessitate a different look. Recognising that he had a tremendous run of hair form, from looking futuristically ahead of his time in the 1960's to being bang on trend from '71 to '79, he decided phase out of the game, although he didn't officially stop until 1985. Terry Neill was sacked in 1983, as we languished near the foot of the table. The Irish days were well over by then, but a new era was beginning to emerge of young London boys who would come together to form the best teams of George Graham's era. Just a few weeks before he got the boot, Neill gave a debut to a lanky 17 year centre half who would become the bedrock of Arsenal for the next two decades: Tony Adams.

Fast forward to 1996. When Arsene Wenger joined the club there wasn't any Irish culture anymore. Steve Morrow, the only Irishman at the club within a sniff of the first team, was swiftly shipped out. If there was a culture at Highbury, it was a drinking one. However, with his modern regime that espoused the benefits of moderation, stretching and broccoli, Wenger set about instilling a culture at the club that reflected his own experiences and ideas from French football. This was accompanied by a steady stream of French imports. Already reeling from the signing of Dennis Bergkamp by Bruce Rioch, the fans didn't know what to make of the appearance on the scene of Remi Garde and Patrick Vieira. Next came Nicolas Anelka, Emmanuel Petit and Gilles Grimandi and, er, David Grondin. Later still rolled up Thierry Henry, Sylvain Wiltord and Robert Pires. And most of these players were destined for the first team. While Arsene did buy players from other countries with some success (Freddie Ljungberg, for example), his dabbling in the homegrown market was less assured. Take a bow, Franny Jeffers. We became less English, and it's fair to say that at this time Arsene Wenger used his knowledge of French football to put his ideas into place.

With so many Frenchmen around the place, there was a decidedly Gallic air to Highbury, helped of course by France's success at the World Cup in 1998. Arsenal supplied the world champion's midfield, after all. 'Allez les rouges" urged the Jumbotron on match days. "He's quick, he's blonde, he's won the Coupe du Monde", went an adaptation of the Petit chant. There were even rumours of *soupe du jour* being served in the North Bank. It was all much more overtly French than when similar numbers of Irishmen had been at the club: back then you wouldn't have been able to get a pint of the black stuff to go with a bowl of champ.

The balance hung between being all out continental and retaining some British-ness. Arsenal had become less 'English' in the eyes of the media, who welcomed Arsene when he arrived with the tolerance and openness for which the British press is famous. They ran a smear story about him. Even other managers stuck the boot in: "What does he know about English football?" sneered Alex Ferguson, who was then forced to eat his words as Arsenal won the double. But while Arsenal retained their famous all British back five, it was still possible to see the shift in culture. We were becoming just a bit different to other clubs, although they, too, were opening the doors to more foreign players, if not yet coaches. But Arsenal were changing the fastest, and it was visible not just in the names on the teamsheet; results went our way too. Fitter, more skilful and pacy, the French revolution was plain to see when we took the field.

Not that this was all plain sailing. There was often a background crackle of xenophobia. When Patrick Vieira went on a formidable run of red cards, it wasn't long before the fact that he was French was levered into the equation, as if this provided an insightful explanation for his dismissals. "I could smell the garlic on his breath", squealed Neil Ruddock, after Patrick gobbed on him on his way off for an early bath. In later years, Thierry Henry would be accused of having Gallic arrogance, although, in truth, he did suffer from a nasty bout of taking himself too seriously. One of the more risible ideas was that the new, French, Arsenal wouldn't like it up them. The spirit of Corporal Jones was alive and well (and still is, these days it divides its time between the homes of Sam Allardyce and Tony Pulis). Yet the duo of Vieira and Petit soon scotched this idea as they put together one of the most effective midfield partnerships ever seen. When one of them was out, there was always Gilles Grimandi, the duffle-coat wearing assassin who saw red at the Nou Camp for elbowing Pep Guardiola and got himself banned at Lazio for drawing blood from Diego Simeone. Even in retirement he showed he still had it, scything down Edgar Davids in Dennis Bergkamp's testimonial, then giving an insouciant shrug. Check it out on YouTube – it's well worth it.

The Frenchness of Arsenal probably reached a peak somewhere in the end of the 1990s, when the players we had were on the way to their peaks, the World Cup was under their belts and Bergkamp had just finished the best season many people have ever seen from an Arsenal player. Throw into the mix our poetry and jazz-loving captain, the erudite manager, and Highbury was beginning to feel like a left bank collective. Would we get rid of the match day programme and have an artistic manifesto instead? Would the team run out one day wearing polo necks, puffing on Gauloises Disque Bleu, indulging in a bit street theatre? Not quite; but we were unmistakeably changed from the Arsenal of the preceding years. Even after Petit left, the Pires/Henry axis ensured our French flavour persisted. Great players both, they particularly seemed to aggravate the spiteful hackers like Wise and Bowyer, who ran around in a state of frothing aggravation whenever we played them. Having been lauded as some of the finest English talent, it must have been particularly rage-making for them to real-ise that, actually, they weren't that good. To have your face rubbed in it by a Frenchman, of all things, and one with elaborate facial hair, was simply too much to bear.

Since those invincible days, the French empire has declined a bit, but it hasn't fallen completely. It's not for nothing that Arsenal are sometimes called the biggest club in France. We've still got a French manager and French players, even though with Clichy going this summer Diaby is now our longest serving one – although it feels like he's only played about five times. But, as the spending and youth policy has developed, we've become less French and more global, if that's the right word. We don't have the singular feel we once did. These days we have players from all over. Where before Arsene relied on players he knew from French football, now he relies of youthful potential, no matter where it comes from. Still, it's not hard to see that a group of players from one nationality could come to dominate places in the first team. It could even be British; Walcott, Ramsey, Wilshire, Gibbs, Alex Oxlade-Chamberlain, could all form the core of the first team in the next few years. Who knows? One thing that is clear is that the shared French culture at Arsenal helped, for a few years, to make us the best team around. Let's hope that a similar thing can happen again, wherever the next group come from. Hell, even if they're all from Iceland I'd gladly eat a rotted shark roll at Ashburton Grove if they win us the league.

Skál!

Jonathan Swan is the red and white sheep of a Spurs supporting family – he had to share his room with his brother and a life-sized model of Glenn Hoddle. He now writes about Arsenal as a kind of therapy.

23

ON THE ARSENAL BEAT

JOHN CROSS

For a club known as the Bank of England, it was a period of immense change. After George Graham's departure, Stewart Houston, Bruce Rioch and Pat Rice all took charge for brief spells at a club known for being stable, traditional and loyal. Arsenal were not used to the kind of scandal that went with Graham's exit after he admitted taking a bung. His book's title, 'The Glory and The Grief' said everything about the two sides to his memorable reign. But next was to come an even bigger change for Arsenal – the club's first foreign manager in the guise of Frenchman Arsene Wenger.

I've had the opportunity to work with all of them for either my first paper, the Islington Gazette, the club's programme or magazine, and then later the Daily Mirror. My path did not cross so much with Rioch but I was fortunate enough to have seen all the others at close hand; from my days as a young reporter covering the youth team with Rice and then later with his brief stint as caretaker boss. Houston remains charming, still does scouting work for the club and I see him about from time to time. He's a nice man, has a great football brain and yet his time in charge after stepping up from being Graham's assistant took a massive toll on him. Then, of course, there's Wenger who, in my opinion, is the greatest manager the club has ever had and, taking resources into account, is the best manager in Premier League history thanks to his vision, methods and style of football. Fortunately, in a book for Arsenal fans you don't have to defend that accolade too much, but I sincerely hope supporters do remember it amid the leanest spell of his 15 years in charge. It has been a genuine pleasure to cover Wenger and his Arsenal team. He is charming, warm and brilliant with the press. And, even more importantly, his teams play great football and have had great success. Wenger's era came after some highs and lows with George Graham who, for a young reporter, could be a very intimidating figure. But Graham was great for me and I will always be grateful to him.

I first started covering Arsenal when I was a teenager on the Islington Gazette – a dream job for someone who grew up on the North Bank. Graham was also a dream. Long before the days of the new super hi-tech training ground at London Colney and Arsenal having a press officer, everything media-wise was done through George or his secretary, Sheila. Arsenal's state-of-the-art training base these days is a world away from what London Colney used to be like. A pokey little hallway next to the treatment area, with the changing rooms to the left. It also used to be home to youth games and some reserve games. But that environment made someone like me feel incredibly close to the heart of the matter.

The great thing about George was that no reporters were allowed to the training ground – apart from me as the local paper reporter; the guy from ClubCall (remember that?) and I would often double up to do the programme, too. The occasional foreign reporter was allowed in to pander to Graham's ego. He enjoyed the thought of being well regarded overseas. Graham would often complain (like many managers) that English papers wouldn't want to talk tactics like the Italians. But if you enquired as to whether Anders Limpar (a luxury player in his eyes) could fit into the system that would quickly end any conversation. Graham was a successful player for Arsenal, a member of the 1971 Double winning side and remembered the Gazette when he came back as manager. That's why he offered us special privileges. If I wanted to speak to a youth team player then George would have to give the green light before Pat Rice would let me. Pat was incredibly strict and protective, while the reserve team manager, George Armstrong, was one of the nicest men I've ever met in football. I would stand in the doorway of the little ramshackle training ground, next to the medical room – if you could call it that – and grab the players as they came past. It's a million miles from that now, but it allowed you to build up close working relationships with players and staff, some of who are still there now like chief scout Steve Rowley, and others who have moved on such as Steve Burtenshaw.

There were characters, too. Martin Keown always enjoyed some banter, Tony Adams, David Hillier, Ray Parlour and Stephen Hughes also spring to mind as characters from that period. But, in reality, it is Graham who stands out in my mind. He could be great company but incredibly sensitive about articles – to the point of pinning some things up in the dressing room to motivate players. He also had an fierce temper. Fortunately, I didn't upset him too often, although one such occasion still springs to mind. One Sunday newspaper had made allegations about him accepting a bung and yet he still found the time a couple of days later to ring and complain about a story I did – about the youth team. Graham was very protective about his young players. At the time, Stephen Hughes was seen as the next big thing. Comparisons to Liam Brady had been made and this really upset George. That is probably why he reacted badly and rang to tear a strip off me for reporting that he had been given an unprecedented long-term professional contract. Quite amazing when you consider that he was in the eye of the storm about bungs, and that it also came at a time when the team and the club had been rocked by various scandals, including Paul Merson's booze and drugs confession. It was after revelations about Merson that Graham went into lock-down mode. For the first time ever, I was turned away from the training ground. Bung scandals could be blowing up and yet George's first concern would be about his players.

Waiting in marble halls for Rice and Armstrong was also an education. Pat Rice is deservedly an Arsenal legend, and his link between past glory, the history of the club, and the present is, in my opinion, priceless. Wenger has embraced Rice as a touch of British grit in a multi-cultural environment. Don't knock it until you remember that he was at the heart of unique glory at the club; The Invincibles season, glorious football and trophy after trophy in the first part of Wenger's reign. Rice has always had a drive and determination that made him get the most out of his talent as a player. You will also get very few niceties out of Rice. He's a straight up and down football man whose first thought is football rather than PR. I often stood in those marble halls for an hour, an hour and a half, waiting for a couple of minutes to talk to Pat for the programme. You do it as a reporter. Forget press conferences. That happens at Premier League level. But those times spent in the marble halls meant you got talking to people. Youth team players, reserve players, directors, scouts and players who were to go on to become agents, pundits and writers when their playing careers did not work out. They were great times. There was a buzz when you saw a player develop. You formed little relationships and under-standings. Now there's a wave of former Arsenal players in the media like Ray Parlour, Paul Davis, David Hillier and Stewart Robson who I remember from 20 years ago. These days it's so different. And it's a shame that those relationships have been ebbed away.

It's hard to imagine that there will be characters like George Armstrong at Arsenal again. After reserve games, he'd come out to the marble halls, summon me into the coaching room, talk football, introduce me to football people and make me feel comfortable with the likes of Steve Burtenshaw or Steve Rowley. People would come in from scouting missions while I was there. Not a word was ever spoken or written by me about the players. It was all about trust and they were terrific times. Then after being made to feel truly at home in the coach's room, Geordie (as Armstrong was affectionately known) might offer me a lift home if I wasn't driving. There are some nice people in the game. Funnily enough, I think of Sammy Lee in that way. I did a PR stunt with Umbro in 2004 ahead of the Euros. Lee took the session. Afterwards in the dressing room, he noticed a whacking great scar up my back from an opera-tion. It was something of a conversation starter. Now, I'll see him about on the circuit and he's so genuine, a real charac-ter, a truly nice guy. That's what George Armstrong was. If there's anyone with a bad word about the late great Geordie then I've yet to meet them. That was the old Arsenal.

There was a brief period in between that and the Arsenal of today. Stewart Houston was unlucky enough to fill in for a brief stint with the first team. Houston's spell came after George's sad demise for the bungs scandal. Stewart oversaw a European campaign, a difficult end to a season and all the time maintained a great dignity. After all, George had been his boss. He took his programme notes far more seriously than any other manager at any level. I often did the programme notes with him. He wanted to think about his message to the fans, the message he wanted to get across and cared what they thought of him. Stewart is a man who deserves a lot of credit for the way he conducted himself at Arsenal.

Rice and Rioch had brief spells in charge. One of the great little known stories about Wenger is that he nearly got the job a year before he arrived in 1996. David Dein championed Wenger, the board were reluctant to appoint a relative unknown Frenchman ('Arsene Who?' was the headline when he finally took over) and a year passed before he came in 1996. This happened during a spell I worked with an evening paper in Swindon to further my career as a journalist. It was good trying to get a back page lead every day out of a 30 second phone call to Steve McMahon. I like Steve and we have a laugh about those times now. He can't believe I've gone from Swindon Evening Advertiser to Daily Mirror: I struggle to believe he's not in the English game anymore. His passion was unquestionable and, despite some ups and downs, I like him and still run into him and some of his old players and staff. That's the thing as a journalist; it can be chance meetings or contacts along the way that really help. Back in those early days I got to know David Dein. He was a fantastic servant for the club; I still admire him, and still regard him as a master fixer. From players to manager, he made some great deals for Arsenal. So it was a very happy coincidence that, back in 1998, as a freelance in some European outpost, I turned up again to cover an Arsenal pre-season friendly. Thankfully, David was there to make an introduction to me with Arsene Wenger. Not that it mattered or probably registered with Wenger, but it did with me.

Wenger remains a genius in my eyes. He treats everyone the same. He very rarely calls any journalist by their first name, although, I am assured, he knows who exactly the regulars are. Occasionally, very occasionally, he's called me the magic word: John. Most notably at the Football Writers' Association tribute night held in his honour (and people say that the media is on his back! We love him). I went up to the top table, congratulated him and asked him to sign my brochure for my wife. Sadly, she piped up it was for me which he found hilarious. For the past few years, I've covered Arsenal regularly. There have been ups and downs but the respect remains the same. If you see him in a lift or a car park at an international tournament, he will always stop, talk and make small talk. It's never about who Arsenal should sign or so on. It's about having a chat, him being a nice, down to earth man with charm and humour. While Arsenal's Colney base was being refurbished a hotel near St Albans was his second home or office. On a couple of occasions, I ran into him there. He'd always engage, stop, chat and even share a drink. He's warm, humorous and great company. For years, after his press conferences, we would have a separate chat with him in a private room. He'd talk French politics, holidays and life. Sadly, while us newspapers do get a separate chat with him, the room has gone. So has that intimacy. In my view, it's a mistake. If you like someone, on whatever level, it's harder to criticise. We still respect Wenger, but clever managers keep the press onside. We support him. Even to the point of The Times having a page two leader-column supporting Wenger recently. I still believe he's the right man for the job. But Wenger does not like criticism even though he's happy to debate. He cracks jokes; we crack jokes with him. I think he enjoys good repartee with us.

When he turned 60, I presented him with (what I thought anyway) an expensive bottle of wine from the regular Arsenal press troops. He was grateful, respectful and thankful. The sadness is to see him struggling. These have been difficult times. Sadly, he sees it as a problem driven by the media. I will always maintain that it's not the media who are chanting on the terraces to spend some money. The good thing about Wenger is that you can have a chat about things. When he got upset about a headline last year, I spoke him after a press conference, tried to thrash out the problem. There's no doubt that he's trying to scale back on his press stuff. That's a shame; Arsenal, for many years now, have been an example to most as to how to operate in the media; for player access, interviews and the manager. Not only did they get good coverage for their success, the media liked covering them. It shows. Honestly, every fan thinks the media has it in for their club. They remember the bad headlines, forget the good headlines and say the papers have it in for their team or manager. For every bad result and bad headline, under Wenger, there have been ten glowing write-ups and count-less pull-outs and specials after title wins and successes. Try topping the Daily Mirror's 'Arsenal Win The World Cup' in 1998! Wenger rarely gets upset, really upset anyway. One occasion springs to mind. Jose Mourinho accused Wenger of being a voyeur, having a telescope and looking over the fence in jealousy at Chelsea. One of my broadsheet colleagues pushed it and pushed it. "Do you have a telescope, Arsene?" "No, really do you?" Many have never seen him so angry.

The great thing about Wenger is that he will take any question. We don't duck questions and he doesn't duck answers. Anyone who stands on the steps of his new club to deny unfounded Internet rumours is clearly someone who will not shy away from an issue. From that day forward, Wenger made a point of limiting one-on-one interviews. He rarely gives them. But he will often joke that we have his number we can call him if necessary. Again, he's always polite, respectful and friendly. The man oozes class, respect and manners. But things do upset him. Like the time a back page had him dressed as a tramp, when he said he wouldn't go to Real Madrid even if he was on the street. But, again, I was happy to have a chat and he ended up laughing about it and we all moved on. He can have a furious temper. You see that in press conferences and behind the scenes sometimes.

Often on European trips you see each other at close quarters, in hotels or on the plane. But, in more than 20 years of covering the club, Wenger has provided more great times, highs and success than you could ever imagine. The Bank of England has become a very different place; Silent Stan, a chief executive with a background in the MLS, but more than anything else, a French manager. That is a departure from the Graham era and beyond. However, these have been great times and people will miss him when he eventually goes. Wenger has brought a touch of tradition, class and style to Arsenal that has only strengthened the club's standing within the game. This achievement, together with great football and success, should never be forgotten.

John Cross is a football writer for the Daily Mirror. My Dad brought me up to be an Arsenal fan. Now I just get told: 'I thought you were supposed to be an Arsenal fan' whenever I have to report when they've lost. You can't be both.

24

A NEW ARSENAL: BUILT ON
A BELL LANE DYNASTY

NIGEL BROWN

"What does this Frenchman know about football? He wears glasses and looks more like a schoolteacher. He's not going to be as good as George Graham...can he even speak English properly?" said Tony Adams upon a certain Frenchman's arrival, in his autobiography, 'Addicted'.

There is a piece of video that perfectly depicts 'The Arsenal' ethos pre-Arsene Wenger. It is a bleak Monday morning on the 12th November 1990, and we have just been deducted two points following a mass brawl at Old Trafford, mainly thanks to nutty Nigel's fisticuffs with Brian McClair and Dennis Irwin. Despite the handbags, we won the game 1-0 in what proved to be a defining moment in a season that culminated with the League title returning to Highbury.

Outside London Colney, the training ground Arsenal shared with University College London, the players gathered, summoned by George Graham following the news of the tribunal hearing. The backdrop is a tired old-people's home of a training facility, a threadbare squad, the shortest Adidas shorts that would make even Kylie blush; topped off with a rousing speech from the Scot that centred on getting the fans on-side, creating a siege mentality, and proving the 'Arsenal hating media' wrong. This methodology was very much the Arsenal way. We worked hard, we were together; it was Arsenal against the world. While professional on the pitch; off the pitch there was a good old-fashioned British football culture that required George's disciplined approach. From the Tuesday Club, eating competitions on the bus home (Merse was the king), and the staple pre-match fry up, it was a mix that created a unique team spirit, forging an ideology for the club's players and fans alike.

The training ground actually belonged to UCL (University College of London), with Arsenal paying for the privilege of its backward facilities since 1961. But we were not alone; the likes of Tony Adams, Perry Groves, Terry Neil, and Liam Brady trained alongside the students themselves. My sister, who attended the University during the early nineties, recalls the Arsenal boys, led by Merse, watching a university lacrosse match, chanting from the sidelines, egging on the young ladies.

The original site is now used by Watford FC, and has not changed a great deal. There is still a lack of security, with cars able to drive up to the training ground car park, while back when Arsenal were tenants it was even used as a venue for some inappropriate behaviour – though this time it had nothing to do with the players. Terry Neil recalls a car park tale from his autobiography. "I remember a large builder's van parked in this curved entrance, then a small car (badly) parked just beyond it. Veering around both vehicles, I noticed the builder sat in his van, with a woman on his lap, their arms wrapped around each other, locked in an embrace. I mentioned it to the staff when I parked up, and apparently the driveway was sometimes used as a meeting place by locals needing some privacy with nowhere else they could safely meet."

The facilities themselves left much to be desired for a club with a rich heritage like Arsenal. The dressing rooms were too cramped to fit the whole squad, with players having to spread to other changing rooms across the complex. The main pitch, exclusively used by Arsenal for 'closed door' friendlies, and the South East Counties youth team, was adjacent to some farmland, (which is now Watford's main first team training pitch). Arsenal's pitches, used by UCL during the week were clay-based, and a constant victim of poor drainage. Training was regularly moved to the indoor plastic pitch and gym behind the Clock End at Highbury when they had fallen foul of the English weather. Essentially the clay-based soil meant Arsenal's training ground was more suitable for grazing sheep than a Championship winning side, so it isn't surprising we adopted the long ball on occasion.

The fire at London Colney in the mid-nineties forced Arsenal players to change in a hotel and train at Highbury, while the youth team changed out of Portacabins at Colney. A backdrop that had been the breeding ground for Charlie George, Liam Brady, Paul Merson and Tony Adams, was now far behind the rest of Europe. With the introduction of Arsene Wenger things were set to change, and quickly.

The landscape of football was also changing, with new money, increased competition and the formation of the Premier League. When George got his brown envelopes confused in 1995, it was time for a drastic change at a football club stuck in the dark ages. Suddenly there were new facilities, a change in diet, a modern structure, and a new style of play.

We had been successful under George Graham, but never world class. Following the 1991 league win, the club never again challenged for the title under the Scot. David Dein wanted to modernise Arsenal, keeping the professional approach that the club was built on under George, but nevertheless, install new forward-thinking principles at the club. In the summer of 1995 the club appointed a short-term ticking time bomb in Bruce Rioch who, despite clashes with Ian Wright and co in the dressing room, guided the Gunners to a respectable sixth-placed finish. A much-needed season of stability following Graham's fall from grace, heralded the arrival of Dennis Bergkamp and David Platt, marquee signings we were certainly not used to.

However in the summer of 1996, following England's exit from Euro 1996, Dein was able to convince Wenger to join us, causing all the old school stalwarts to react in shock at his disposition. You've heard it all before about Wenger; described sneeringly as a maths teacher, then his utter the cheek for subbing Tony Adams in his first match in charge at Borussia Mönchengladbach, followed by his refusal to speak at half time. Oh, how he has changed.

Wenger's appointment was announced on August 20th, but he didn't meet the press until September 22nd (he actually took official charge on September 30th, a Monday morning). "He arrived unnoticed at the training ground," Lee Dixon famously said. "A meeting was called, the players filed in and in front of us stood this tall, slightly-built man who gave no impression whatsoever of being a football manager."

Adams in particular had his doubts. "There was a feeling of who the fuck is he and what is he going to do? What is he?"

Little did our Tony know that Wenger's vision on how a modern football club should be run would influence the likes of Manchester United, Liverpool, Barcelona, and Real Madrid, and have far reaching consequences for the future of professionalism in the sport. Bob Wilson, goalkeeping coach at the time Wenger was installed, and eventually one of his greatest advocates and friends, recalls the first time the Frenchman arrived at the training ground.

"I was sitting in an office at the old training ground we used to lease when in walked Arsene. I remember him saying 'I do not understand. This is Arsenal? It cannot be Arsenal'. First in his sights was a new training ground, purpose-built and paid for in an ingenious way. He bought Anelka from Paris St Germain for £300,000 and sold him to Real Madrid for £23 million. From that, £12m created the country's best football training facility. And with the spare £11m he went out and bought another young French player called Thierry Henry. Some business; some brain."

Wenger had a master-plan following years of amassing an encyclopaedic knowledge of football from spells in France and Japan. With the keys to a football club entrenched in tradition and values gifted to him, our new Gallic leader had the perfect blend of ingredients to put his philosophies into action. Joining him was right hand man, Boro Primorac, and a team of French medics, including Yann Rougier, a specialist in dietary supplements (who had previously developed a remedy to enhance sexual performance), his assistant Hervé Castel, and osteopath Philippe Boixel.

The most immediate changes focused on diet and the application of science to training. Out went favourites like ham, egg, and chips, and in came raw vegetables, steamed fish, boiled chicken, and pasta without the sauces. Wenger never forced this on his players. The benefits soon became obvious, particularly during the Premier League run-in of the 1997/1998 double-winning campaign, where we were noticeably stronger as the season reached its climax.

Training was meticulous. Wenger would give his signal–two minutes to go – during a game of five-a-side. The time would pass without an outcome until Arsene picked up the ball and call, 'end of session.' Wrighty, bursting with energy, might protest, 'next goal wins gaffer!' but Wenger never broke his measured and controlled programme.

Plyometric stretching was also introduced which benefited the elder statesmen and extended their careers, with many of them extending their careers far longer than the Frenchman believed possible. The stretches were compared to the rack by some of the old guard, painful, but when followed correctly, produced long-lasting effects that ultimately allowed Dixon, Winterburn, Bould, Keown, Adams, Seaman, and even Bergkamp, a few successful extra chapters.

But the training complex was Wenger's primary concern. He wanted his Mecca of modern football facilities, and his own legacy to be built. Wenger had more or less the final say on all specifications. Firstly, because the board believed in him following the immediate double-winning success, and secondly, because he had clear plans in place, plans he had failed to get off the ground during a seven-year spell at Monaco. The architectural design was based around natural elements, lots of wood and natural light were crucial, and absolutely no mud being allowed in the centre, with players, staff, and visitors having to take shoes off on entrance to the complex. This was an influence from his time in Japan, where an obsession with hygiene emerged. Wenger built a "dirty room" between training pitch and changing-rooms as players were not allowed to sully the inner sanctum. Immediately players would change into flip-flops, dressing gowns, and enter state of the art changing-rooms that took inspiration from the American locker rooms of the NFL. It was a place of Zen-like tranquillity and calm, surrounded by state-of-the-art facilities and techniques.

Wenger insisted six changing rooms were built, intelligently splitting the first team and youth team between two different ends of the complex, with one corridor peeling away to the first team, and the other to the youth set-up; intended to make players think "one day I will walk the other way", with each corridor adorned with a photography of some of the greatest moments in the club's history. A swimming pool was built with an adjustable floor and viewing gallery, with Wenger being one of the earliest adopters of the theory that muscular tears and tissue damage could be monitored better in water. While a state-of-the-art gymnasium, massage rooms, treatment rooms, and restaurant were built, in the same area as the restaurant, an area for relaxing was installed, complete with ergonomic sofas purposely designed to prevent slouching. Wenger even insisted that the traditional red and white colours of the club would not adorn the training centre; instead calming pastels and neutral off-whites were chosen.

On average, around 70 footballers use the training facility every day, while at the weekend, the centre stages youth team matches as well as reserve team friendlies. Under the watchful gaze of head groundsman, Steve Braddock, ten full-size pitches complete with under-soil drainage and an automated sprinkler system, are kept in pristine condition; two of them have additional under-soil heating. Each pitch is built to the exact specifications of the playing surface at the Emirates Stadium, with Wenger insistent that conditions should mirror match-days as closely as possible.

Despite its impressive facilities, the Bell Lane development faced heavy opposition due to it being a Greenfield site; the board had to enclose letters of support from then England manager Glenn Hoddle and Barcelona manager Sir Bobby Robson. Ken Friar persuaded the pair to back the project; letters enclosed alongside planning applications to Hertsmere Council, outlined why the facilities would benefit the future of the national side – an argument backed up by the emergence of Jack Wilshere and Kieran Gibbs and given further credence by England's regular use prior to every international.

With the sale of Anelka and planning permission granted, Wenger now had the go ahead for the most advanced training centre of its kind in the football world. But Wenger continued the development of the facilities and training methods. The Frenchman pioneered the first use of Pro Zone and GPSports (now standard across international and

Premier League clubs). The performance analysis product, GPSports, allows Wenger to evaluate performances in training and real-time during matches thanks to the biometric 'bra' players are made wear under their shirts. While ProZone was the first electronic software of its kind to record specific post-match and training data, such as yards covered, number of passes completed, as well as a host of other intricate statistics, including scientific data.

And he hasn't stopped there, with further plans to develop the training ground once more already underway, including a state-of-the-art 'Desso' pitch, like the Emirates surface, and the addition of 'AlterG' rehabilitation technology – a progressive innovation to help players recover from training and injury, with Nike having invested heavily in the company. The results have been impressive in the NFL in the United States; Wenger is of the belief that it will aid and speed up rehabilitation time significantly.

Wenger introduced a biological and scientific side to training that is now standard across Premier League, Champions League and international set-ups. He was the first; he alone raised the bar for other clubs to become more professional. The far reaching effects of his philosophy have culminated in a new Arsenal, with a modern 60,000 seater stadium, one of the best academies in the world, topped off with being a sustainable club, superbly run, and one renowned for being among the great entertainers in world football. If we look back to dogging in the car park, sausage and mash post match, and 5-aside behind the Clock End, it is simply chalk and cheese.

Wenger is solely responsible for a revolution. No wonder the board gave him the skeleton key to the club.

Nigel Brown launched and edited Sport.co.uk. His first Arsenal game was a 1-0 home defeat to Manchester United in 1992 and he has been a season ticket holder ever since. His favourite player of all time is 'Captain Fantastic' Tony Adams.

25

MR F

NICK AMES

The door is slightly ajar when I knock, as it so often is. Ken Friar OBE must have looked out of his office window, or perhaps even walked out onto his balcony overlooking Drayton Park, hundreds of times – surveying the sweeping, poignant panorama of the new Highbury Square development that these days greets his every sideways glance. Now, though, he's facing squarely the other way and watching the screen of his Mac. It's August, a particularly busy month in modern-day football, and the man still regarded by all and sundry as 'Mr Friar' shows absolutely no sign of letting up. Almost to the day, this is the start of his 62nd year on Arsenal's permanent staff. When you add another five or so as a temporary employee, he's been a cog – of every size imaginable – in the Arsenal wheel for comfortably more than half of the club's 125-year existence. Nobody has embodied the Gunners' tradition, and its concurrent moving with the times, as adeptly or as selflessly even if, as he puts it with characteristic self-deprecating humour, "I'm still looking for a regular job!"

If the club's rate of change during the first half-century of his employment could be described as stately, the last decade's developments have been positively supersonic; it's rarely been easy and has, as he tells me, often been plain exhausting. The warmth and wit remain, though, as does the twinkle in his eye as he recounts just some of a wealth of Arsenal experiences that will, surely, never be matched.

The beginning seems a very long time ago now, but can we start there? The story of how your involvement with Arsenal began is well-told, but remarkable, and bears repeating.

It's honestly not a story I'm proud of, just one of those things than happened and I suppose you can't alter history. I was a young boy and, as boys did then, we were playing football with a tennis ball outside the stadium on Avenell Road. The ball rolled away, and I ran after it as it disappeared underneath a big car. I scrambled under it, trying to rescue the ball, when a voice boomed out: "Boy, what are you doing?" I was scared to death! It turned out to be George Allison, the manager at the time. For some reason, he then told me to come back the following day. Why I obeyed him, I have no idea even now – it would have been easier to run away, and that would have been the end of it. But I returned as directed, and that's how it all started.

So you went back - and then...

I went back and saw him - he introduced me to the box-office manager of the time and I then started as managing director! No, I began on half a crown a week running messages from the front door to the box office on a match-day. I was at Highbury County, a local grammar school, so this was something extra. But believe me, I still have no idea what made me come back.

But message boy to managing director is still an incredible leap. How did the progression work from there?

When the time to leave school arrived I had various things on the table. I wanted to be a stockbroker, and there was a position with a firm that I was really keen on taking. Five years had passed since I first started working at Arsenal, and the Club had been onto my family saying they'd like me to come and work full-time. My parents agreed, but

I wasn't keen because the salary I'd been offered at the stockbrokers' office was twice as high – another £1.50 a week – as I'd get at Arsenal. Eventually they won, and I started here as a full-time employee in 1950, on £78 a year. From there, I worked through all kinds of departments. The business was very different then, remember – even when we were still over at Highbury in the early 2000's, we only had one hundred and nine staff. That's nearly quadrupled now.

From then, your rise was – in its understated way – meteoric...

Well, it was steady. I first became a bit more involved at boardroom level in 1965 – the club secretary was the big job back then and I was made his assistant. I moved up to become secretary in 1973; then became managing director ten years later. I stayed in that position until a time when I very much thought I'd be playing golf, and ended up deeply involved with Danny Fiszman and the move to Emirates, as you know.

Does the growth you spoke of just now astonish you?

I sometimes sit back, yes, and think of the way the club has changed and evolved. But remember, Nick, you've grown up in a period when everything is there. Back then we had no photocopiers, for example. Any reports had to be, typed and if there were twelve copies the girl had to do each one three times with carbon papers. I would produce reports and it would take me perhaps a day to do a report I could now write in five minutes.

Another example for you – tickets. Every ticket was produced by a printing company. They'd arrive in books and then had to be checked physically against the seating plan. Then you'd sell them over the counter and people would queue to buy them from the front entrance in Avenell Road up the hill, down the hill, right along to the tube station – thousands upon thousands of people, when it was a big game. We did all that on very few staff, but now it's unfathomable to people.

And that's just part of it – then there were the other areas of the business. Players used to get one-year contracts, there was a fixed salary and every year you'd renew all of the contacts in one day! We didn't have massive numbers of shareholders or much of a commercial operation – instead we had lotteries that made us a £1000 a week and that felt like a fortune. We eventually had the highest shirt sponsorship deal around, with JVC, for over £100,000 a year and that was a big thing in its day. The scale of things has changed immeasurably.

With that, business practices themselves have moved on. Is it less about the bonhomie now?

It always has been, and still is, very cordial, but you have to remember that, although the bonhomie you mention was always there, the Club was still run like a business. The likes of Sir Samuel Hill-Wood and Sir Bracewell-Smith were both big businesspeople; Denis Hill-Wood was a senior partner in a stockbroking firm; Peter Hill-Wood was vice-chairman of a bank; Sir Chips Keswick was chairman of one. So it's not been all "What's next old chap?" – far from it. Once that door shuts it's very much a business affair. In the boardroom it's always been "Chairman" and "Sir" even if we're on first-name terms, and are very good friends, outside it.

I count twenty major trophies in the cabinet since you started here. It's such a broad question, but have any been more satisfying than others?

It's hard to talk about any in particular; there have been so many events, memories and successes. I suppose one had to be the 1970/71 'double' because we'd not won anything since 1953 – we'd endured seventeen years with nothing and suddenly started to win things. That was enormous and such a great satisfaction. There was also 1989 at Anfield of course. But tomorrow's match is always the most important – that's a maxim I always stand by.

Seventeen years with nothing perhaps puts the current run into perspective. But it leads me to ask you whether there

have ever been any particularly dark periods in the years here – times when you thought the outlook was bleak.

There have certainly been times where you think the light's been switched off, yes. But, honestly, it's always been a great place to work and it's the sort of job you wouldn't be able to do unless you absolutely loved it. It's more than a nine-to-five – the demands can be huge. I remember we'd be working over eighty hours a week regularly, for nearly six years, when we were working on the new stadium. I remember Danny once asking: "Do you feel tired?"

I said, "I do, a little bit," and he then told me we'd worked eighty-seven hours that week. So that, in particular, was a very challenging time.

We were starting meetings at lawyers' offices at 8am and I'd sometimes put my key in my lock back home at six-o'clock the following morning. My son was living with us at the time as his house was being decorated – one morning I gingerly put the key in the door so as not to wake anybody. He came down the stairs and asked "What time do you call this?!"

It was exactly what I'd been saying to him all his life.

That's astonishing…

Well, for me it's been a privilege. I've been so lucky to be involved with a club like this. We've worked as a team, we've had a great unit off the pitch and it's always been 'we' rather than 'me'.

The 'we' includes countless memorable characters from down the years, of course – does anyone in particular spring to mind?

I remember an old guy that worked in the ticket office when I first started – somebody came in and said they'd like to buy two seats for the weekend and asked if there would be a post in front of the seats. The chap said sternly: "Sir, I would remind you that our stand is supported by voluntary contribution only!" There were so many characters like that that maybe you wouldn't get today. Then there were people like Denis Hill-Wood, Peter's father – he was a great personality and loved by everyone, a real part of the Club's fabric. And there are the ex-players, too, those who keep coming back and being a part of that we do. We still see the 1970/71 guys on a regular basis for example, and others from down the years too. Arthur Shaw is now 84 and he still comes in regularly. That affinity, that love, really counts for something.

And then, of course, there was Danny…

A phenomenon. What he did was phenomenal. He gave up so much, and probably lost a lot of money personally, in devoting the same eighty-odd hours a week – bearing in mind he had quite a big business to run too. He was utterly devoted to the Club, loved it – he'd wear the same red socks to every match through superstition, and we went to every game together home and away. He was a great, great character and a lovely, lovely man.

What makes Arsenal, the club of which you are such an enduring symbol, differ from others?

It's the people that make the Club. The fans make it, the manager makes it and all the people that work for it make it. We have a set of values that I think are treasured, and we should never lose sight of those values – they were laid in place some eighty or ninety years ago by the Hill-Wood family and have been perpetuated ever since. I suppose if I'm to take credit for anything it's for playing a part in continuing those traditions. Tradition doesn't pay the wages but it's a very important part of the structure, the fabric, of the Club.

Here's an example. In 1939, players going off to the war were granted bonuses of £500 – a big thing back then. These bonuses were to be loaned back to the club at two-percent, so actually they never got the money. That came to light in the early 1980's – the chairman found out and I was told to go back and find as many of these ex-players as we could. We then compounded that money and paid them some forty years on. That's one real-life instance of the values we seek to live by.

The number of managers you've worked with here is in double figures, but you and Arsène have been particularly close...

It's been a great time. He's good at everything, one of those people you wish you hated! We were once in a meeting with people of four or five nationalities and he just kept changing languages effortlessly. Once or twice he's shaken me – we might have a relatively obscure player recommended and he'd reel off the chap's full professional and personal details off the top of his head. We were in Spain recently and he knew twenty of the players on the teamsheet, everything about them. He has a phenomenal football brain and can discuss any other subject you like with remarkable aplomb. I've travelled all over the place with him and he's never lost his temper with anyone! It goes without saying that we've been so lucky to have him, and the day he decides to leave us will certainly be one of the saddest days.

On the other side of this corridor, it's possible to look out onto the bridge that was named after you last year. Could you ever have imagined it?

It's a bit embarrassing; I'll have to catch the people responsible! We'd planned what we'd do to commemorate Danny, then the meeting was stopped and an addendum announced that a decision had been made to name the second bridge after me. I don't even remember what I said at the opening ceremony – but I think it was along the lines of "when I started I thought the only thing they'd ever name after me was a coat-hanger." Needless to say, someone gave me one of my very own with my name on it the other day! But it's incredibly flattering to have a bridge named after me – now I just need planning permission for a toll at either end of it!

And as you cross that bridge daily, walking between Highbury House and the stadium, do you feel that you have as much energy as ever?

Well I've cut back now; it's just sixty hours a week! No, I'm still here every morning before 8 – I try not to stay into the evening as the pressure isn't there to do so. But look, I work because I love the place and the people. I still get a great kick out of it, and am probably the luckiest guy alive to still be doing what I've always loved to do.

The interview reaches its natural conclusion, we say our goodbyes and instantly, after shutting the office door on my way out, I hear Mr Friar returning one of the calls he's evidently missed during our conversation. Six hours of the working day still remain; not a second will be wasted, because not one ever has been. The landscape upon which his labour of love sits may have changed forever, but a man whose term of service extends well beyond the combined ages of Theo Walcott, Jack Wilshere and Alex Oxlade-Chamberlain is not planning to wind down any time soon.

Nick Ames is a journalist for Arsenal Football Club

26

WE'RE ON OUR WAY

ANDREW ALLEN

"We can be proud ... we can be so proud."
Thierry Henry, 17 May 2006, Paris.

In the 24 years that I've been watching Arsenal, I have
come to realise that there is no uniformity in the way one
deals with defeat. There have been results that have left
me fuming with anger and frustration, beatings that have
moistened the eyes, setbacks met with casual shoulder
shrugs and losses confronted with gallows humour.

Defeat to Barcelona in the 2006 Champions League
Final, however, stands alone. Perhaps it was the romantic
Parisian setting, or maybe a hangover from the sentimen-
tal farewell to Highbury just days before; but where pain
should have pulsed through my veins in the aftermath of

Juliano Belletti's winner, there was instead pride and an unadulterated sense of belonging.

Yes, Arsenal had fallen at the final hurdle, but the manner in which the race had been run up to that point was nothing short of heroic. Deliciously dynamic, nail-bitingly ugly, robust, exhilarating and so often gut-wrenching; the twelve games on the road to the Stade de France had come in all shapes and sizes and seen minnows and giants banished alike.

THE FINAL FAREWELL

From the moment a date was set for the move to the Emirates Stadium, the countdown to an emotional Highbury send-off became an unavoidable reality. After 93-years making a home betwixt its glorious Art Deco facades, few expected to walk away from their favoured turnstile without a tear or two. Acknowledging the importance of tipping collective caps at the achievements of days gone by, and recognising the merchandising potential of paying respect to Highbury's history, Arsene Wenger's men were kitted out in a commemorative redcurrant home shirt which echoed the strip sported by their antecedents of 1913.

As reigning FA Cup champions and with the record-breaking 49 game unbeaten run still fresh in the memory, expectations were high that domestic success would add an extra gloss to proceedings come May. Regrettably, it was not to be so. While Highbury remained a fortress in the league until mid-December, a poor run of away results proved to be the club's downfall. By the New Year thoughts of winning a 14th title had been supplanted by worries that neighbours Tottenham Hotspur might pip the club to fourth place in the table.

CONTINENTAL SALVATION

It was therefore to the continent Arsenal looked for salvation. Awaiting them in the group stage, Swiss side, FC Thun; Dutch giants, Ajax; and Czech outfit, Sparta Prague.

While qualifying for the Champions League had posed little problem during the Arsene Wenger era, progressing past the quarter-final stage had proved nigh on impossible. Valencia and Chelsea took turns to dash hopes of European glory when momentum seemed to be building in 2001 and 2004 and making that even more painful for Arsenal fans was the fact that both Manchester United and an unbelievably gutsy Liverpool side had both claimed the big-eared trophy either side of two Premier League coronations in North London. While a sense of entitlement grew year-on-year, so too did the pain of inevitable let-downs. It almost felt like the club had developed a kryptonite aversion to success in Europe's premiere knockout competition.

There was little sign of an end to the malaise as the Clock End timepiece struck 9.37pm on 14th September 2005.

Down to ten men in the first group game against Swiss minnows, FC Thun, and with the scores locked at 1-1, the Gunners looked nothing like potential competition frontrunners. That was until substitute Dennis Bergkamp tenaciously wriggled free in the penalty box, lost the ball, retrieved it and calmly slotted home to seal three morale-boosting points in the third minute of injury time.

Having sold the talismanic Patrick Vieira to Juventus during pre-season, Thierry Henry and Gilberto Silva struggling with injuries and Jens Lehmann and Robin van Persie suspended, there was a makeshift look to the spine of Arsenal's side by the time they visited the Amsterdam Arena for the second group game versus Ajax. Luckily, the depth of Wenger's squad saw him able to call on 'Invincible' stalwarts Robert Pires and Freddie Ljungberg; both of whom netted on the way to a creditable 2-1 win. We didn't know it at the time but Markus Rosenburg's reply for Ajax in the 71st minute was to be the last goal conceded for 995 minutes.

COMETH THE HOUR, COMETH THE MAN

Struggling with a groin injury for the majority of the first two months of the season, Thierry Henry had been treated with kid-gloves by the Arsenal medical team. However, eager to ensure progression to the knockout stage by securing the magic nine-point marker as quickly as possible, the striker was a surprise inclusion on the Gunners' bench when Wenger's patched-up side travelled to the Czech Republic to face Sparta Prague. Having scored a brace against Fulham in late August, Henry spent a full six-weeks frustratingly sitting one short of Ian Wright's 185 goal scoring record. As expectations mounted in the press and on the terraces, there was great hope that like Wright before him, the landmark would be reached in front of a packed Highbury.

It wasn't to be quite so poetic, but that isn't to say that reaching and surpassing the milestone in Prague was devoid of a quixotic edge. Unsheathed from the blankets of the bench to replace the injured Jose Antonio Reyes in the 15th minute, Henry put in one of those individual performances that to this day makes the hair on the back of your neck stand up. Socks rolled above his knees, the gloved musketeer reclaimed the captain's armband from Gilberto and set about his business with gusto.

Inside four minutes he made his mark. Superbly controlling a long ball by Kolo Toure, he swivelled on the edge of the Sparta box and in one balletic movement curled an unstoppable shot into the back of the net with the outside of his right foot. The pitch-level camera angle did the goal particular justice, capturing the swerved path the ball followed around a defender, as it veered outside the left-hand post and dipped with pace past the keeper. It was a superb effort and indicative of the quality Henry had demonstrated since arriving from Juventus in the summer of

1999. He thumped his chest with pride and glared with his trademark Gallic haughtiness; it was goal number 185.

In the second half, his scowls turned to beaming smiles. Even 'Titi', ever the coolest of cats, wasn't able to mask his joy at becoming Arsenal's greatest ever goal-scorer. Receiving a delightful through ball from his partner in *va-va voom*, Robert Pires, he bore down on goal with two defenders to his rear and the Sparta keeper racing off his line. Having scored from similar scenarios countless times before, he was never going to miss and calmly slotted the ball home with the aid of a slight deflection. Well aware of what he'd just done, but also conscious that the moment may have slipped the attention of others, he beckoned his teammates to celebrate with him. They were all too happy to pass on their congratulations.

That the historic brace was scored against a Sparta side sporting a redcurrant strip, directly inspired by the one which Arsenal had themselves revived to celebrate their final season at Highbury, added a tasty garnish. It was one of those nuances of circumstance that so often pepper football almanacs, but are all too often forgotten.

FORWARD

Three wins out of three became four out of four when Sparta were swept away on their return visit to London. Henry again got on the scoresheet while Robin van Persie, developing a reputation as something of a super sub, bagged two in a routine 3-0 victory to secure safe passage to the knockout rounds with two games to spare. The win was the first time Arsenal had recorded four on the trot in continental competition for over thirty-years, but it still didn't guarantee top spot in the group. A late Robert Pires penalty in Switzerland finally did the honours as plucky Thun were downed 1-0, before a drab 0-0 draw against Danny Blind's Ajax confirmed that the Gunners would progress to the knockout rounds unbeaten for the first time ever.

Despite indulging in the best run of European form since 1972, there was little optimism in North London that this particular Arsenal side would be the one to break the club's Champions League duck. The squad was stretched to the limit with the much maligned Manuel Almunia and Pascal Cygan both forced into action and youngsters such as Gael Clichy, Emmanuel Eboue, Alex Song, Philippe Senderos and Mathieu Flamini all blooded in place of the injured Lauren, Sol Campbell, Ashley Cole and Gilberto. Even the likes of Kerrea Gilbert, Seb Larsson and Quincy Owusu-Abeyie garnered first team minutes.

When the draw for the first knockout round saw Real Madrid's name pulled out of the hat, there was a forlorn sense that such youthful exuberance could be found wanting. Indeed in the month before travelling to the Bernabeu, Everton, West Ham United and Liverpool all beat the Gunners in the league, while a defeat to Sam Allardyce's

Bolton Wanderers meant there would be no successful defence of the FA Cup; it was a painfully bad run of
domestic form and made everyone fear the worst ahead of
a clash with the reigning Spanish champions.

AGAINST THE ODDS

Amazingly all fears of a trouncing at the hands of the
'Galacticos' proved unfounded. Whatever wise words
Arsene Wenger imparted to his team ahead of the first
leg, they seemingly worked wonders as his side produced
a near pitch perfect performance in the Spanish capital.
The 4-5-1 formation, introduced to provide more midfield solidity away from home, proved as fluid as any of
the performances achieved with the previously favoured
4-4-2 set-up. Gilberto Silva expertly swept up trouble in
front of defensive pair Philippe Senderos and Kolo Toure,
Alex Hleb and Jose Antonio Reyes provided energy on the
wings, while Freddie Ljungberg and Cesc Fabregas were
the creative hub, charged with providing ammunition for
Thierry Henry.

Inside the first two-minutes Reyes forced a fantastic save
from Casillas. Minutes later a terrific tackle from Roberto
Carlos denied Ljungberg. Henry then headed wide from
six yards. They were three terrific chances and the clock
hadn't even reached ten minutes. Marvellously, Arsenal
didn't relent and by the time the referee signalled for half-

time there was a genuine sense that the Gunners had the momentum to become the first English side to win in the Bernabeu.

Two minutes after half-time Cesc Fabregas, who had expertly dominated proceedings, calmly fed a pass to Thierry Henry. From the centre circle he drove like a raging bull towards the Madrid goal brushing off Ronaldo, Guti and Sergio Ramos before sliding a left foot strike across Casillas into the bottom corner. Across the world Arsenal fans reacted with jubilation as they indulged in replays of a breathtaking goal by a Gunner Galactico in one of football's most famous cathedrals.

Ljungberg, Pires and Abou Diaby all had chances to double the lead in the final minutes as the pocket of travelling fans mockingly chanted, 'adios, adios, adios,' at the despondent and departing Madridistas. When the final whistle blew, the sight of Philippe Senderos in a lengthy embrace with the legendary Raul seemed to sum what had just happened. It was a genuine underdog victory.

With a slim advantage to defend in the second-leg at Highbury there was fear that Arsenal might retreat into their shell, sit deep and try and hold out for 90-minutes. Mercifully, it wasn't to be the case, as the most exhilarating 0-0 draw ever witnessed at the old ground came to pass. Both sides attacked with guile and quick interplay, last gasp tackles were in abundance, the woodwork was shaved then rattled; shots were blocked by any means possible.

The game, played against the backdrop of an electric atmosphere, had everything – everything that is – but a goal. In the main that was thanks to a superb late save by Jens Lehmann who commando-rolled across his Clock End six-yard box to deny Raul when the Spaniard's mishit shot looked destined for the back of the net. It was a fine demonstration of athleticism by the eccentric German and ensured victory without the need for extra-time. The Gunners marched on, goalless but glorious.

COMING OF AGE

Two days later Arsenal were paired with Juventus in a mouth-watering quarter-final tie which saw Patrick Vieira inevitably dominate the pre-game headlines. It had only been eight months since Arsene Wenger sanctioned the sale of his protégé and the pairing felt somewhat inevitable despite the towering midfielder remarking: "At times destiny serves up some surprises."

Running away with the Scudetto (although they were later to be stripped of the victory as part of the Calciopoli match-fixing scandal), Fabio Capello's side represented formidable opponents. Bolstered by the arrival of Vieira, Juve could also call on Gianluigi Buffon in goal, Fabio Cannavaro and Lilian Thuram in defence, Pavel Nedved and Emerson in midfield and strike options including David Trezeguet, Adrian Mutu and Zlatan Ibrahimovic.

Despite the stellar cast, the only name spoken about in the aftermath of the first leg was that of Cesc Fabregas – it was without question a coming of age performance. Utilizing two years spent learning from Vieira on the training fields of London Colney, the 18-year-old Catalan skewered his old mentor like a matador in the bullring. He ran the midfield with impish authority, always showing for the ball, relentlessly eager to link-up play for his teammates and providing an end product which all but won the two-legged tie inside 90 minutes.

Six minutes before half-time a tackle, as crunching as it was rare, saw Robert Pires dispossess Patrick Vieira and lay a ball into the path of Thierry Henry. Surveying his options the striker picked out a darting Fabregas who with his first touch controlled the ball, with his second teed up a shot and with his third dispatched the ball through Thuram's legs and past a flat-footed Buffon. He wheeled away in celebration almost surprised at his own brilliance.

In the second half, the diminutive maestro returned the favour for Henry. Racing through the Juventus defence from a deep midfield position he latched onto a perfectly weighted pass by Alex Hleb before cutting the ball across the box for Henry to double the lead. Game over and the Italians went into self-destruct mode. First Vieira was booked and subsequently banned from the second leg before Mauro Camoranesi and Jonathan Zebina were each sent off.

It didn't get much better for the Turin giants in the return leg; the crumbling Stadio delle Alpi a fitting home for a side whose European aspirations were eroding by the second. In cruise control Arsenal, having amassed seven consecutive clean sheets in the Champions League, never looked likely to give away their two-goal cushion. Seeing out a 0-0 draw, achieved with a minimum of fuss and demonstrated a level of maturity, boded well for the semi-final fixtures against La Liga opponents, Villarreal.

FANCIED FOR THE FIRST TIME

Having vanquished Ajax, Real Madrid and Juventus – three of football's great aristocrats – a semi-final showdown with a club making their first appearance in the Champions League was not so much underwhelming, as it was disconcerting. Given Arsenal's travails trying to surmount the European football ladder, there was certainly no room for underestimating Villarreal. Tough opponents, with a distinctly Latin feel, the Yellow Submarines had come third in La Liga to qualify for the competition and subsequently helped knock out Manchester United before eliminating Rangers and Inter Milan. Counting seven players from South America (including the mercurial Argentine Juan Roman Riquelme and Uruguayan hot-shot Diego Forlan) they were dangerous on the break and tough to break down in the midfield.

The pressure was on and Highbury sensed as much as the last European match ever at the grand old arena kicked off. For the first time in months Arsene Wenger's young squad had been tipped as favourites and this sense of expectation triggered a noticeable level of nervousness, despite Kolo Toure giving the Gunners the lead on 41 minutes. As was so often the case, Thierry Henry was the catalyst. Reacting first to a cleared corner, the World Cup winner fed a cunningly disguised pass to Alex Hleb allowing the Belarusian enough time and space to flash a low ball across the six-yard box where it was crashed into the back of the net by Kolo Toure.

While Arsenal dominated possession, the much wanted second goal failed to materialise. Villarreal were denied a stonewall penalty, Riquelme was booked and the home crowd cracked jokes about a squirrel that had made its way onto the pitch only to be greeted by chants of, 'Gooner, Gooner, Gooner.' In the second half Arsenal continued to press but the game petered out with both sides wary of committing too many men forward. It was to be a home win or bust for Villarreal as they settled for a 1-0 defeat in London.

Arsene Wenger promised publicly that the team would go on the offensive when they visited El Madrigal six days later. It sounded good on paper, but when it came to it, the Gunners froze. Quiz any Arsenal fan on what they recall of the first 88 minutes of the semi-final second-leg and they'll no doubt recall nothing more than a torturous yellow blur and frantic action in and around Jens Lehmann's goal. Time after time the Spaniards attacked and time after time they spurned chances to equalise. Then, just as it looked as though Arsenal might close out the game, the referee awarded an incredibly harsh penalty against Gael Clichy for a nudge on Jose Mari. All and sundry knew that if Villarreal scored they would win the match in the resulting extra-time.

The responsibility of taking the spot kick fell to Juan Roman Riquelme. As the television cameras zoomed in to capture the moment, three times they focused on the Argentine's face before he finally, after what seemed like an eternity, stepped up to take his kick. It was impossible not to recognise the look of utter fear in his eyes. When the Argentine finally made contact with the ball it was immediately apparent that Lehmann had outfoxed him. Diving to his left the athletic German parried the ball back past his adversary before Sol Campbell stuck out a leg to put an end to further danger.

It was football at its most cutthroat, a timeless 'heroes and villains' moment. For Lehmann there was sheer jubilation; for Riquelme it was a nightmare that to this day he admits was, "one of the saddest moments," of his career. Crushed by the miss the Villarreal players could no longer muster the energy to close down their opposite numbers and when the whistle finally sounded many were inconsolable. It was Arsenal's night.

24 hours later Frank Rijkaard's Barcelona ground out their own 1-0 aggregate victory versus AC Milan to ensure that they would be the opponents in Paris. It was the final the continent craved.

PARIS IN THE SPRING

In the eyes of the wider football fraternity, the roller-coaster journey to the climax of Europe's premiere club competition finally elevated Arsenal to an echelon which for so long under Arsene Wenger the club had strived to reach; while for supporters, it provided further evidence of forward momentum at a time when Art Deco opulence was being traded for towering modernism.

Ten days before the showdown in the French capital the curtain was finally drawn on 93 years of Highbury drama. The sun shone, flags were waved proudly, legends paraded, the pitch was flawless, Thierry Henry scored a hat-trick, Champions League qualification was secured (at Tottenham's expense of course), speeches were made, the clock ticked down, fireworks exploded and tears were shed as a capacity crowd, decked out in red and white, said their poignant goodbyes. It was a fitting final salute.

While a homely 38,359 had witnessed the end of an era in N5, it was estimated that over 50,000 Arsenal fans made the journey to Paris for the final on May 17th 2006. It was nothing short of an invasion. Around the Eurostar terminal at Gard du Nord, the streets heaved with Arsenal vendors and excited supporters who readily exchanged lager and chips for pomme frites and bière. Given the Anglo-French connection Arsene Wenger had fostered during his decade in charge, even the locals seemed supportive of an 'English' win. The biggest match in the club's history encouraged a carnival atmosphere, although as lucky ticket-holders bid au revoir to those who had to make do with local pubs, nerves began to take effect.

Could Arsenal really beat Barcelona? Was this finally the end of the wait for European glory? Unfortunately and heartbreakingly, it was not to be. On a night of torrential rain, Lady Luck finally chose to sever her ties with the club on whom she had doted so much in the preceding eight months.

With Georg Frideric Handel's "Zadok the Priest" still ringing in the ears of the 80,000 crowd, Thierry Henry twice went close to giving his side an early lead. In familiar, hometown surroundings he played like a man possessed, desperate to recompense the Arsenal contingent in what seemed destined to be his last match before a summer switch to, of all teams, Barcelona. Despite toiling relentlessly his misses in both halves were to prove costly, although arguably not as damaging as the red card shown to Jens Lehmann after 18 minutes.

Penalised by referee Terje Hauge for felling Samuel Eto'o on the edge of the box, the goalkeeper received his marching orders despite Barcelona willingly slotting the loose ball into the back of the net. While his teammates called for the goal to stand and the German to be reprieved, there was little that could be done when the official chose to apply the letter of the law. It was an uphill battle after that, even though Sol Campbell raised hopes by thumping home a powerful header to give Arsenal an unexpected half-time lead.

As the clock slowly ticked down, Barcelona finally and inevitably imposed their game on the Gunners. In the space of five minutes the one-nil advantage was overturned. First substitute Henrik Larsson freed Eto'o to slide an equaliser inside sub Manuel Almunia's near post, then the Swede teed up Brazilian Belletti to drive home the winner with only nine minutes remaining. Arsene Wenger's side had been gunned down and with no energy left to expend and lactic acid burning their muscles they limped to the final whistle, unable to muster a response.

Initially stunned into stony silence by the cruel result, the Arsenal fans soon regrouped and found their collective voice. Over and over they cried, "Ar-se-nal, Ar-se-nal, Ar-se-nal." It was a magnificent and devoted outpouring of passion at a moment when sullen contemplation seemed the only natural course of action. Against the cacophony of Cockney hollering, a bitterly disappointed Thierry Henry remarked, "We can be proud, whatever happened tonight, we can be proud." He couldn't have been more right. It had been a tremendous season and one that augured well for the future. Barcelona were champions, but Arsenal were winners as well.

If success is measured not by arrival at a final destination, but by the spirit and endeavour laid bare while undertaking the journey, then the European adventure of 2005-06 certainly lived up to the club's motto: Victoria Concordia Crescit.

In the 125-years since Arsenal was founded, it remains the closest the club has come to being crowned Europe's best side. To have been part of the experience was an unforgettable privilege.

Andrew Allen is an occasional sportswriter with a lazy disposition. He recently founded The Arsenal Collective, which may or may not still exist by the time of publication. He cringes at talking about himself in the third person.

ACKNOWLEDGEMENTS

I'd first like to thank all the contributors to this book, without whom it couldn't have happened. Obviously. I laid this on them in the summer and to a man/woman they reacted with enthusiasm and interest, and kept to the really tight deadlines (most of them!). With their talent and passion for the subject matter they have made the process as simple as something like this can be.

Thank you to David Rudnick for his outstanding design skills and wonderful cover, and to Saltwater for working so well to a incredibly tight schedule.

To Mrs Blogs for being Mrs Blogs but also for her fantastic editing skills. Thankfully she wasn't as punctilious when choosing a husband.

To Blogette for not making tea. To my brother, the Mugsmasher, and my father Terry, for all their help in the last 12 months. You guys are aaaaalll right.

Finally, a big thanks to you, reader of this book, and, I assume, reader of the blog. I've been writing Arseblog for nearly ten years. As much as I love to do it, it's your comments, your emails and all your interaction that make it all worthwhile.

From one website has grown a truly unique community, both online and off. I guess I shouldn't be at this stage, yet I remain consistently amazed at the generosity and decency of Arsenal fans towards each other. I think of those who travel from near and far – sometimes very far indeed – to find themselves welcomed with match tickets, beers and great company. This happens not just now and again, but constantly.

Arsenal brings people together, forges friendships, camaraderie, loyalty and so much more. At a time when it's easy to dwell on the negatives this most positive of aspects ought to be recognised. I'm glad Arseblog has played a small role in this.

For whatever reason we support Arsenal, be it family, nationality, falling in love with a great team (or a not so great team), or even if we have no idea how we came to be a fan, we should always count ourselves lucky to be fans of this wonderful club.

We support The Arsenal but, never forget, we are a big part of what makes The Arsenal so great.

Andrew Mangan
December 2011